NO INSTRUCTIONS NEEDED

An American Boyhood in the 1950s

By
Robert G. Hewitt

Illustrated
By
The Author

ArbeitenZeit Media

NO INSTRUCTIONS NEEDED:

An American Boyhood in the 1950s

Text and Illustration by Robert G. Hewitt

ArbeitenZeit Media
P.O. Box 74
Trade, TN 37691
rights_info@arbeitenzeit.com
404-287-0715
Find us on the Web at www.arbeitenzeit.com

Kindle Edition ISBN 978-0-9843780-0-5
Trade Paperback Edition ISBN 978-0-9843780-1-2
Trade Cloth Edition ISBN 978-0-9843780-2-9
Printed and bound in the United States of America

**In Fond Memory
Of
My Long-Suffering Parents
June and Buster Hewitt**

TABLE OF CONTENTS

TABLE OF CONTENTS - CONTINUED

The events described in
this book are true.

Many of the names have
been changed to protect
the innocent and enhance
the legend of the guilty.

ABOUT THE COVER:

The photograph on the cover is of the author, age 12,
at a Scout campout.

INTRODUCTION

Ah, the Internet. Provider of so much that is good and useful. Messenger, also, bearing news perhaps left best unknown, like this tidbit. My old high school is gone – bulldozed, razed, knocked down, and generally plowed under. It probably took all of the above to subdue it, for it dated from the late-1920s, a prime era for durable educational construction.

I won't be hypocritical and shed crocodile tears over its ruins. High school was not the most-interesting time of my life. Even so, I feel a little guilty, suspecting as I do that lingering traces of my years-long obsession with its destruction, of wishing it would crumble around me, ending forever the need to endure any longer the tedium and frustration, the creeping and dragging by of time, may have contributed to this dusty ending. Still, at last, I've won, for I'm here and the school is gone.

At the same time... at the same time, the news served to pull me back, to another age, another place, to years of post-World War II optimism and (in the eyes of a kid at least) reassuring predictability. I didn't really want to go there, but I did, pen and paper in hand, laptop on standby. And you know something? It's true what they say. The past *is* another country, and boys *did* do things differently there. It was a lot of fun.

ArbeitenZeit Media

CHAPTER ONE

OUR NEIGHBORHOOD

The neighborhood was suburban, about three miles west of town, a tidy enclave of mostly late 1920s and 1930s houses, many – like ours – in a picturesque style euphemistically known as "English Cottage" or even (depending on how grand the speaker feels at the moment) "English Tudor." Most of the houses were roughly twenty-eight by forty feet, situated on lots not much larger, around sixty by 100. The houses sat to one side of their lots to leave room for a two-track concrete driveway leading to the rear of the lot where a small, narrow garage waited. All the lots backed onto an alley that ran east-west.

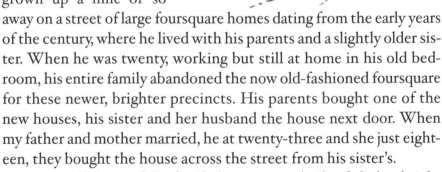

My father had grown up a mile or so away on a street of large foursquare homes dating from the early years of the century, where he lived with his parents and a slightly older sister. When he was twenty, working but still at home in his old bedroom, his entire family abandoned the now old-fashioned foursquare for these newer, brighter precincts. His parents bought one of the new houses, his sister and her husband the house next door. When my father and mother married, he at twenty-three and she just eighteen, they bought the house across the street from his sister's.

All three of the family houses were built of clinker bricks with mortar that looked as if it had been troweled on in gobs and been allowed to harden with no more than cursory raking. All the houses had steep roofs, round-topped wooden doors, and tall, peaked chimneys. Those with raised stone terraces at the front that were part of what amounted to a porch had over that section heavy canvas canopies held up by iron spears angled from the front of the house. At least one of the houses with the suggestion of an actual porch had, instead of the usual railing, a heavy-linked iron chain that drooped elegantly between iron posts set into the tile and concrete floor. Inside, the walls were of roughly troweled plaster, the living rooms had brick fireplaces with heavy mantels, and the wood moldings at floor and ceiling were appropriately substantial. Decoratively, the houses were appealing, inside and out, but many were small, like ours, with just a living room, sunroom, dining room, kitchen with breakfast nook, two bedrooms, and a bathroom. They could also be inconvenient, given that their heating system consisted of a coal-fired furnace that required not only regular tending but also the storage of fuel. In the end, they proved too small or otherwise inadequate for the rest of the family, who sold out within a few years and moved on, but my parents stayed, settling more or less comfortably into this neighborhood that had been so recently carved from a landscape of century-old farms.

It was an attractive neighborhood, for quite a few trees remained, mostly oaks, towering over the houses, shedding their leaves in irritating profusion and without any regard for the obsessively yard-proud homeowners below who had to deal with the result. The trees provided the only note of physical spontaneity, for the developer had adhered strictly to a regular grid when laying out the area in the late 1920s. Our neighborhood's part of it was a rectangle, roughly three east-west blocks by six blocks north-south, squared off at the southern end but slanting to a triangular point at the northern. Within this area of approximately one-half by one mile, the east-west streets had names that paid homage to inventors, saints, a university, and the state. North-south streets were numbered, with the numbers decreasing toward the north. All the roads in the actual neighborhood were paved in concrete with prominent curbs, but there were a couple of undeveloped patches of land just east of the area that were intersected with gravel tracks. About two-and-a-half blocks to the west of our house, still in the neighborhood but in the part left unbuilt until after World War II, the development petered out into woods fronting a stream whose northeast / southwest track for a long time formed the neighborhood's western boundary.

The neighborhood was convenient. There was a bus stop at the end of our street, just a couple of doors away, with a service that ran every half-hour in both directions. Next to the bus stop was a one-story, concrete-block building housing a scaled-down grocery store with just two checkout lanes but at which you could buy most of what was available in the regular stores as long as you didn't expect much in the way of brand choice. Adjacent to the store was a small dry-cleaning pickup stand. Four blocks away was a combination gas station and market. A cluster of services was available at The Point, a big five-way street intersection also about four blocks from my house, including a grocery store, hardware store, pharmacy, barber shop, florist, shoe-repair shop, beauty shop, barbecue joint, type-writer-repair shop, service station, and general-repair shop, where people took things like appliances that needed new cords, radios that hissed and crackled, and lamps that would no longer work.

It was three-quarters of a mile to a hospital, across the street from the foursquare in which my father grew up, and a mile to another major intersection that centered an area containing a dentist, one of the biggest churches in the area, a movie theater, a café, two five-and-dime stores, and the area branch of the city's public library, a handsome Carnegie-funded structure in a vaguely Georgian style with imposing steps leading upwards to a columned porch.

The grade school I attended was only three blocks away from our house, no more than a fifteen-minute walk even if we dawdled, which was usually the case. The grounds of the high school sat on the far side of the grade school, adding maybe another block and a half to the walk. The Presbyterian church we attended was a drive of no more than five or six minutes. The state fairgrounds, a favorite destination when something was going on, were maybe a mile to the west.

On our block, counting both sides of the street, there were nineteen houses. Most had been built at the start of the development, in the same style and of the same size and general plan as our house. The only exceptions were a somewhat larger house at mid-block that sat on a lot and a half (owned by probably the most-prosperous family on the street) and three newer infill houses, one of which also occupied a lot and a half. The larger house was English Cottage in style, its back yard ambitiously landscaped with a courtyard, fish pond, and even a walkway that meandered elegantly among its carefully tended flower beds. The infill houses, all dating from the late 1940s, were smaller and built of wood in a simple ranch style.

The occupants were mostly nuclear families, with parents in their thirties and forties, the father the breadwinner, the mother a full-time homemaker, and a couple of kids of school age. The exceptions were a retired couple whose children were grown and living elsewhere, a divorced woman with two sons, a childless war widow, and the wife of a man who'd retired early because his drinking made it impossible for him to hold a job.

The men on the block represented a range of occupations: the owner of a small store; a train engineer; a salesman of heavy industrial equipment; the president of a syrup-manufacturing company; an accountant; and a manager at the steel mill. The next blocks over were much the same, save that there were a few school teachers, a security manager for the local Railway Express Agency (the father of my best friend), and the head teller for one of the bigger banks in town. The one divorced woman managed the lunch counter at the big downtown Sears store. The war widow was secretary to the manager of a downtown movie theater. The retired drunk's wife was the bookkeeper for a local real-estate company. My mother, neither widowed, divorced, nor in dire need, broke the norm for female employment in that she always worked, partly, I'm sure, because she and my father appreciated the extra income, but mostly because she enjoyed her jobs, which involved managing drug stores and gift shops.

The neighborhood was homogeneous and generally apolitical, essentially Anglo-Saxon in its genealogy and middle-class American in its values. All the men of draft age had served in the Second World War, and a woman up the street, before her marriage, had been a WAC. Probably 60 percent were regular churchgoers, mostly Protestants, with Baptists and Methodists in the majority, many of whom attended not only Sunday morning and evening services but also the Wednesday night prayer meetings, the men in conservative suits, white shirts, ties and – occasionally – hats, the women in nice dresses, hats, gloves, pumps, and (in winter) a wool coat often topped by a fur stole, dragging along kids wearing their churchgoing best. The 40 percent who weren't so assiduous in their religious observance offered acceptably respectable excuses and usually made it a point to stay indoors until after Sunday lunch.

The neighbors were as consistent in their vehicle choices as in everything else, with the most popular automobiles being Chevrolets, Fords, Oldsmobiles, Hudsons, and Buicks (the make my parents had come to favor).

Some of the residents – like my parents – enjoyed a night out, dining and dancing and trying the latest cocktails. Everyone went to the movies on a fairly regular basis, especially for particular favorites like John Wayne, Bob Hope, Jimmy Stewart, Gary Cooper, and Lana Turner (who strongly resembled my mother). A handful of the men bowled or played softball. Some of the women were in the garden club or did volunteer work with the PTA.

At night, pre-TV, the adults would listen to the radio, shows like *Arthur Godfrey and the Talent Scouts* and *Ernie Ford*. When the kids got to choose, the dial would be turned to *Hopalong Cassidy*, *The Lone Ranger*, or *Buck Rogers*. Many of the neighborhood men would listen to baseball games at night, including my father, who would sit stubbornly by the radio until the bitter end, no matter how long that might take. In the mornings, a lot of the women were fans of *The Breakfast Club*, a mixture of music and comedy starring Don McNeill. Even my mother tuned in as she got ready to go to work.

By the end of 1951, most families in the block had their own TVs or were to get them in the coming year. Radios began to be turned on less frequently as the adults kept track of the nights when highly rated TV shows were on, like *Your Show of Shows*, the *Colgate Comedy Hour*, and *I Remember Mama*, the heartfelt tale of a Norwegian family in San Francisco tackling life, felt by most boys to be the height of sappiness.

On holidays and weekends, the big thing was to take the whole family on a picnic to some local park, of which there were several, including a large state park on the southern edge of town. When this became tame as children grew older, some families opted for commercial swimming lakes with slides, special diving platforms and food concessions. In other families, the big treat was a half day at a local amusement park where younger children rode the Merry-Go-Round and pedal boats and older kids stood in line for the Tilt-A-Whirl, Flying Scooter, Caterpillar and other rides whose whole purpose seemed to be to induce nausea. When families went on a real vacation, it was usually to the beach or the mountains, each several hours away. Sometimes they'd visit relatives on farms or in nearby small towns. Each fall everyone went to the State Fair and the Harvest Festival at the grade school. Those with kids in high school sometimes went to the school's football or basketball games.

Among the adults there was a generally accepted code of neighborly behavior. People were relatively restrained, calling each other "Mr." and "Mrs." until they became friendly, when they would usually go to a first-name basis unless one of the couples was much older. There were few close friendships formed, one exception being that between my parents and the president of the syrup manufacturer. My parents thought he was such a nice man that they named me "Robert" after him, which led to my being occasionally invited to visit his well-landscaped backyard to watch the fish in his pond.

There wasn't a lot of formal socializing but much pleasant sidewalk interaction and back-yard conversation. About the loudest voice to be heard was that of a mother calling her offspring in for lunch or dinner.

Holidays were equally low-key. At Valentine's, parents bought cards shaped like hearts for their children to exchange. At

Easter, in yards up and down the street, the adults would watch while younger kids looked under shrubbery and in flower beds for home-colored eggs to add to their candy-laden baskets. On May Day, parents trekked to the high school's football field, where a large Maypole had been set up, to watch their children cavorting about in home-made costumes (my most humiliating, assigned by my second-grade teacher, was a frog). On the Fourth of July, someone would blow off a few illegal fireworks, and almost all the kids had sparklers. At Halloween, area adults by and large stayed home to hand out treats – the acknowledged kid favorite was any brand-name candy. Popcorn balls, no matter how carefully crafted, were our least favorite because they were sticky and had a way of tasting funny. At Thanksgiving, the same kind of meal appeared on tables up and down the street, save that there would usually be a disagreement or two over the appropriate main course (in my household the debate was turkey vs. ham). In December, neighbors exchanged cards bought in a box with twenty others exactly the same, decorated their trees with tinsel, shiny glass balls, and brightly colored strings of lights several days before Christmas, and then deposited the rapidly browning remnants in the alley for city pickup sometime between the 26th and New Year's. Outdoor decorations were almost unknown save for a family or two who stuck into the cold dirt of their front yards home-made wooden cutouts shaped like snowmen, Santa and his reindeer, or The Three Wise Men visiting Mary, Joseph, and the Baby Jesus.

There were a few exceptions to the generally unexceptional adult behavior. A couple of the women – it was whispered – spent too much time with soap operas and candy boxes and too little on their housekeeping chores. Another had a habit of borrowing too often - a cup of this, a bag of that, even, once, my mother's fur stole to wear to a special event. As thanks for the loans, the borrower would bake cookies and cakes and send them over, but my mother was afraid to let us have them. "If she's no better organized than to have to borrow the ingredients, I can't help wondering how careful she is about how she bakes," she'd worry.

Other deviations were more serious in the eyes of the

neighborhood. A man up the way, retired from gainful employment, would get up each weekday morning and walk steadily a mile or so to a bar on a main thoroughfare, spend the day drinking, and then stagger home at night, occasionally yelling insults at anyone who approached. Another man offended some by the fact that, when he returned from his job, he would retreat to his garage and work on cars, some of the parts for which would find their way into plain view in his back yard, which infuriated neighbors walking by in the alley that ran behind our houses. This attitude was to be expected since the only thing ever out of place in most of our yards were the autumnal oak leaves that persisted (at least until the trees were cut down) in falling onto manicured lawns. My father had a theory about the amateur mechanic – he said working on the cars gave him an excuse to stay busy and out of the house as much as possible so he rarely had to be around his large family, which was – though pleasant and good-looking – boisterously talkative. "It's probably the only chance he has to hear himself think," my father would say, grinning.

For the most part, kids were expected to amuse themselves. This could take some funny turns. One boy, beginning when he was about four, would clump up and down the street wearing his mother's high heels, cultured pearls and a fur stole, primly carrying one of her purses clutched to his chest. No one teased him; it was just accepted that this was the way he was. Nor did we tease his younger sister, who was as butch as he was not and "played boy" in every way she could think of, including helping her father do yard work and fiddling with the family automobile.

Most of us were more traditional, being generally age- and sex-appropriate in our behavior and possessions. All of us had, in turn, some combination of tricycles, pedal cars, scooters, and bicycles. To us, at least when we were younger, a bike was a bike. We weren't fussy, save that no boy would be caught dead riding a girl's bike, which inevitably led to being considered a sissy. All kids had roller skates, the metal kind that strapped over your shoes. This was probably not a good idea in a neighborhood with scored concrete sidewalks, leading as it did to bruises, cuts, scratches, and scabby knees becoming the perpetual lot of the kids on the block. In spite of the hazard posed by the rough concrete surface of the area's roadways, boys played street hockey on roller skates, upping the damage ante. Apart from that, girls and boys tended to play together, usually games like Hide 'n Seek and Red Rover. The girls would sometimes play House, which was also considered a sex-specific pastime, save when someone's younger brother could be coerced into joining them. Before the infill houses were built at the end of the street, the vacant lots served as an adventureland of sorts, where trees could be climbed and all sorts of games improvised. Best of all, someone had nailed a long board into the top of a tall tree stump, and one kid would hang on while another spun her or him around. At the back of the lots, in a clump of close-growing trees, a couple of the more-adventurous of us kids played Doctor, at least until the adults caught on.

Anyone doing much of anything could be sure of being caught out because the stay-at-home moms, going about household duties in their neat housedresses and neatly coiffed, if tightly permed, hair, spent a lot of time glancing suspiciously out windows. It may or may not be totally true that it takes a village to raise one child, but it takes only a few sharp-eyed women to monitor a block full. The second that you were observed doing anything of which it was felt your parents would not approve, the telephone was in hand and your mother or father was being called in order that a full report might be tendered as quickly as possible.

By and large, however, the neighbors were well disposed toward the kids. In 1950, when the Johnsons up the street became the first on the block to get a TV, they invited groups of three to four kids at a time to view *The Lone Ranger* and *Hopalong Cassidy* on the round, twelve-inch, flickering screen of their Zenith.

All of the neighbors were probably more kindly than our behavior merited, and never more so than in the few weeks before Christmas when they would grin and ask us if we'd made up our mind about what to ask Santa Claus for. Most of the kids would blush and shuffle and grin, trying to be appropriately ingratiating in case Santa – ever alert at this sensitive time of year – was watching. Not me. I was wise to the Santa scam, and had been for some time. In fact, by the Christmas I was seven, I was "in on the game," thanks to my parents and their friendship with the owners of the town's largest sporting goods and toy store. It is there, I think, in the back seat of my parents' Buick on that cold Christmas Eve, that I will begin this series of recollections of what it was like to be a boy in that place and time.

CHAPTER TWO

SANTA'S LITTLE HELPER

I began helping Santa at an early age. I think I was about seven or eight. My parents were longstanding friends with the owners of the largest sporting-goods and toy store in the city – Mack's Sports. Every year on Christmas Eve, Mr. Mack Steward would personally deliver sports equipment, especially bicycles, tricycles, pedal cars and scooters, to the homes of his best customers. This was done late in the evening, so hopefully the children of the household would be in bed, which was a reasonable expectation since most kids of the pre-TV era turned in early.

One year my parents were invited to go along on this round of Santa deliveries. My grandmother – who'd lived with us while my father was away in Europe, fighting the War and dealing with its after-math – had returned to her own house, so my previously built-in babysitter was gone. An only child, I had no older siblings to fill in, and my mother wouldn't hear of my being left with a mere sitter on Christmas Eve, when in any event the odds of being able to get one wouldn't have been good. All of which led to the decision to take me along for Mack's late-night delivery run.

I won't pretend I was particularly shocked by what fol-lowed. I suppose I had already begun the pull away from the Santa legend because of my mother's occupation and her inability to keep a secret. She managed a medium-sized drug store and I had been around its premises enough to hear people wanting to put some toy or gift on lay-a-way for "Santa," wink, wink. Also, my mother had a propensity for letting slip little hints of what Santa had in store for me if I was a good boy, which struck me even then as unlikely insider knowledge.

My usual way of selecting what I wanted for Christmas was to get hold of the Sears Roebuck Christmas Toy Catalog. This would be inspected minutely for weeks around Thanksgiving. Items would be circled, then marked out for replacement with others even better. In addition to the contents of the Sears Catalog, my want list always included something from the Lionel Trains Catalog – generously supplied by Mack's Sports. I was already heavily into building my Lionel empire.

I made sure my parents understood what I wanted with no risk of error by leaving the catalogs on the breakfast-room table, open to the best of the marked pages. From time to time, I'd supplement the visual aid by dropping a subtle hint; and when I was really determined to get something, I'd show the page to whichever of them I thought would be most receptive and remark, casually of course, "Don't you think that's the best looking engine (or whatever) you've ever seen?" By this particular Christmas Eve, all the prep work had been done, and I had settled into my Christmas countdown phase, my excitement in no way reduced by my parents' news that I was to go with them. The delivery run would be something different to do while I waited for the arrival of the big morning and, I hoped, everything I'd circled, and I jumped willingly enough into the back seat while my father found a radio station playing Christmas music.

We met at the rear of the store where Mack had preloaded a panel truck with the Santa loot. The order of delivery had been worked out with the store staff, so all we had to do was follow the truck driven by Mr. and Mrs. Steward and help unload the beribboned bikes. This was no chore, for every stop was a mini-party. As the presents were wheeled quietly inside and parked next to stocking-hung mantels, we were regaled with cookies, hot chocolate and, for the adults, a nip of something obviously stronger. As the evening progressed toward midnight, I became more exhausted and sleepy while the adults became jollier and jollier from their "nips."

Some time after midnight, certainly by one o'clock, I was

sound asleep in the back seat of the family Buick, covered with a quilt my mother had the forethought to bring along. That was the last thing I remembered until, somehow, I woke in my bed on Christmas morning, still a little woozy from all the cookies, cake and chocolate from the night before. I then wobbled into my parents' room to announce that it was time to see what "Santa" had brought *me*. This was an era of terrific toys for kids, especially boys. For the most part, I can't remember what year went with what gift except that there was always something wonderful in one of those much-coveted blue-and-orange Lionel boxes. Other highlights included my first erector set – something *every* kid should have, my Red Ryder BB gun, and my first and only Gene Krupa drum set (which disappeared somewhat mysteriously after only a few days).

Christmas was more than presents, however, even for a kid. There were several other prerequisites for the big day to seem authentic. There had to be a real tree with the big colored lights looped round and round toward the spun-glass angel that sat at the very top. We had to listen to Santa on the radio reading letters from kids pleading for the gift of a lifetime. These pleadings were usually hidden in the niceties inserted mostly for the parents, such as "I would like some new school shoes" or "and please don't forget something for my baby brother" and "also some fruit, nuts and candies." The real grabber would usually be buried, often in a postscript like, "Oh, P.S, Santa, please make sure the pony comes with a real saddle."

I enjoyed listening to these poor believers pour out their hearts to "Santa," but I always thought they'd be better off dragging their parents downtown to Mack's, Sears or Woolworth's to focus them on where the goodies really came from. Oddly enough, I may have become a cynical little brat, but the knowledge of the true way of the world didn't interfere for even a second with my enjoyment as I ripped into the bright wrappings on Christmas morning, even if I probably knew most of what I was going to get. It wasn't, after all, the source that mattered, but the fact that what I wanted had indeed at last arrived. I was always a pragmatic kid.

CHAPTER THREE

THE SO-CALLED TRIP OF A LIFETIME

Given that the school year had ended only the previous week and the summer lay in front of me like a basket into which I could put any possibility, I was in a pretty good mood when my mother announced the day before my eighth birthday that she was going to give me my present early. (I wasn't surprised. She could never keep a secret for long.) We were, she informed me proudly, going to California for two weeks!

This didn't seem to me to be a birthday gift. A birthday gift wasn't something you *did* but something you *got* – an erector set, a fire truck, a Howdy Doody puppet, or the longed-for P.T. boat that shot wooden torpedoes. My apprehensions were misplaced. The next day, right on schedule, along with the Cowboy-and-Indian-decorated birthday cake with the stiff white frosting and a card from my grandmother with money tucked inside, I did get the P.T. boat, whose torpedoes worked as advertised, so I was placated.

This California odyssey was not, in fact, a vacation. My mother, the secretary of the Presbyterian church that we attended, was to accompany our minister and his wife to a church conclave in Los Angeles. She could have parked me with my grandmother, who for several years returned each summer to keep me out of trouble, but saw this as a golden opportunity to broaden my education.

"Think of how it'll help him with his Geography," I remember she told my father.

To make this even more special, she announced that we were to be traveling in the minister's brand-new 1948 Chevrolet fastback, four-door sedan. Our itinerary was to take a northerly route west and to return on a southern circuit to vary our travel experience.

I listened to all this in the coming weeks, accepting the regular updates as to route, destinations, and things we might see along the way as no more than background noise to the real business of summer. When someone would ask me wasn't I looking forward to going to California, I would dutifully say that I was and my mother would look pleased.

Time passed, the hours filled with the usual goofing around, often involving the kid-made explosives of one kind or another in which I and my best friend Vernon already specialized. It seemed that summer had just settled into the perfect routine when the day of departure approached and two bags were packed. The big Chevrolet fastback pulled up in front of our house, my father stowed our luggage in its oversized trunk, and we arranged ourselves in the back seat, where the new-car smell was almost overpowering. The minister assured my father that he would take good care of us as his wife smiled politely. My parents exchanged a brief kiss through the open rear window, then the car moved slowly away. I looked back to see my father waving, a big smile on his face. My mother looked equally happy and made some kind of remark about how much we'd been looking forward to this.

And that's almost the last thing I remember clearly about that two weeks. The trip itself is, unfortunately, no more than a very hazy memory. There were no camera buffs along (there are only one or two photos that I recall ever seeing), and none of the grownups appear to have been souvenir collectors. It's a telling commentary on how a kid's mind works to realize the little that I do remember of this two-week period.

Memory One. Somewhere in the Midwest (Kansas, I think). The motel room was home not only to my mother and me but to a trio of happy crickets who appeared to be rehearsing for a regional chirp-along. My mother was up most of the night trying to shoo them out the door or, failing that, stomp them into silence.

Memory Two. Cody, Wyoming. The beds in our hotel room were carved and painted with cowboy scenes, depicting wagon trains, rodeo scenes, and some Indians.

Memory Three. San Francisco. I was sent from the hotel, a few doors down the street, to get my hair cut. My mother said she would be along shortly to pay the barber. When she arrived at the

shop recommended by the hotel staff, she was horrified. She found me sitting next to the door that was not a door but strings of Oriental beads. Above my newly-sheared head hung a calendar obviously advertising some sort of Chinese tonsorial product by way of a smiling flower of half-nude Oriental womanhood. I thought she was very happy among her artistically placed flowers (peonies, I think). My mother thought otherwise. The clerk back at the hotel was thoroughly dressed down for sending such a tender young boy to such a lewd establishment. That was it for San Francisco, the crown jewel of the West.

Memory Four. Los Angeles. The Brown Derby Restaurant *did* look like a hat. I aggravated the hotel elevator operator by constantly riding up and down with him to pass the time of day. I especially remember a jungle-themed restaurant where the flowers and trees were all made from neon tubing – quite a surreal sight. That was all for a five-day stay.

Memory Five. Grand Canyon, Arizona. I don't remember even seeing the canyon – I suppose I did. The only scene that remains is my mother, her fair complexion pink with indignation, becoming infuriated over the one-dollar price for a hamburger consisting of two pieces of loaf bread and a less-than-adequate meat patty. And that's the last of my "Trip of a Lifetime" memories.

When we returned home, Vernon greeted me as if I hadn't been away, and summer took up where it had left off. When school started back and Miss Brown asked each of us to say what we'd done that summer, I think I talked mainly about a model-airplane project that had turned out especially well and only mentioned the California trip as an afterthought. It wasn't deliberate, just an instinctively accurate kid prioritization.

My mother would sometimes say, "Bobby, didn't we have a good time on that trip to California?" I never had the heart to tell her otherwise.

CHAPTER FOUR

DONALD DUCK AND MY MATH PHOBIAS

It was navy blue and orange and shiny, everything a new "official" Donald Duck bicycle should be. It even had a full 3-D Donald head just below the handle bar. From the moment I laid eyes on it, I was enthralled by this wonderful ninth-birthday present from my indulgent parents. Donald Duck was my favorite Disney character. His frustrations, raging temper and lack of self control were traits

that I could totally identify with. I'd wanted this particular bicycle more than anything, but – still in the first glow of my love of trains – I would gladly have accepted instead anything in one of the blue-and-orange Lionel boxes that I had now come to covet. I think if my parents had had any idea of what this "official" bicycle would end up costing them, they would have visited Mack's and bought out the Lionel display. It would have been cheaper.

For two months after my birthday, I had what was until then the time of my life with Donald, wheeling around, in control of my destinations, the envy – I was sure – of every boy who saw me. The sad part of the Donald saga began soon enough, however, in mid-August to be exact. The irritating thing is that I wasn't doing anything silly or wrong, just coasting down my street, headed for the creek about two blocks down. Hearing a car approach from behind, I eased Donald only a degree to the right, but it was a degree too far.

Donald and I hit the curbing, and the hard, unforgiving concrete surface drew us toward it like a powerful magnet. We went down together, my arms and legs tangled up in Donald's handlebar, spokes, and pedals. I ended up on my back, my left elbow somehow trapped beneath me. In extreme pain, I lifted my head and tried to sort out the situation. The driver of the car I'd been avoiding obviously hadn't noticed my fall, for it was almost out of sight. There was no one else around to render aid or assistance. Hurt or not, I was clearly on my own.

It took me a minute or two to get up the nerve to try to extricate myself from Donald's crumpled clutches. Once I was able to stand, I couldn't tell what hurt worse – the skinned-up knees or the left elbow which, now that it was in plain sight, I could see was grossly twisted. The elbow won out. I began the block-and-a-half uphill walk home, crying and cradling my left arm, afraid to look closely at the damage. Luckily about a half block into my trek, Jerry Johnson, a teenaged neighbor fortunately built like a young giant, saw me coming and picked me up and carried me home.

What happened next remains a blur of hospitals, doctors, and a long period of pain and complications. The elbow wasn't dislocated; it was crushed. This led to two operations to insert and remove metal pins (two of which I still have in me today), much physical therapy, and unremovable bone fragments. Then, while in the hospital, I developed a kidney infection which required extensive treatment. When I finally made it home, in mid-October, two months after Donald and I went down, I had the great pleasure of an acute appendicitis attack, which required a return to hospital, another surgery, and still more infections.

By the time all of it, including the complications that seemed to dog every procedure, was over and done with, it was late April, and I had missed almost all of the fourth grade. In the grammar school I attended, unfortunately, that was the grade in which kids were introduced to long division, fractions, and "parts of a sentence." When I returned, others were confidently dividing multiple-digit numbers by other multiple-digit numbers, translating numbers into fractions, and drawing lines on the blackboard showing the relationships between nouns and verbs and verbs and objects, not to mention the roles of prepositions, adjectives, and adverbs.

I was totally at sea. I'm not sure if anyone – parents or teacher – realized that, what with one thing and another, I didn't have a clue. My school record up to this time had been good, so they gave me a pass into fifth grade, assuming I would eventually catch up. I somehow managed to get through that grade and all the others that followed with reasonably decent grades, but fractions, long division, and sentence diagramming remained a mystery. At times, my math phobias almost threatened to overwhelm me, and Donald's wacky, orange-beaked face would rise up to taunt me.

I never knew what happened to Donald. Nobody said, and I never asked. A few months later, when they were sure I was completely recovered, my parents gave me a regulation boy's bike, and Donald receded into memory.

CHAPTER FIVE

THE ROLLING STORE AND OTHER GOURMET MOMENTS

In spite of the elbow debacle, my parents were pretty good about not hovering over me. One thing, however, they continued to insist on: my grandmother would whenever possible stay with me during the summers when I was out of school, to ensure sensible behavior. This never made a lot of sense to me, because my grandmother was babysitting me when Donald and I bit the dust, but attempting to point that out got me nowhere.

My opposition wasn't because I disliked my grandmother. Actually, she was great to have around. In addition to her other merits, she always had some spare change if you needed additional funds – which I invariably did, and she tolerated my friend Vernon in a friendly-enough way, even going so far as to bake him the chocolate chip cookies that were his favorite.

Best of all, she liked to make cakes, maybe my favorite thing in the world to eat. Her cake philosophy was simple: they should be big, tall, and with as many layers as slippage and the laws of gravity allowed. For each cake, she'd bake four regular-sized layers, which she then sliced horizontally and restacked, with a *generous* coating of frosting between each layer. She usually didn't put frosting on the sides. I guess she wanted to show off the towering layers so every one could count them and appreciate the magnitude of her creation. She made many different flavors, but my favorite was a yellow cake with rich butter frosting into which she ground English walnuts. She decorated the top of the cake with more English walnuts, this time in the form of intact nut halves arranged in an enticing pattern. The result was so sweet that my teeth would actually ache.

In reality, I didn't protest her staying with me in the summers because we got along so well, which was no doubt due to the fact that we were complementary in many ways. Because she was deaf, she never complained about how much noise Vernon and I were making. She was heavy and relatively sedentary, and I was rail-thin, a perpetual motion machine. She disliked moving around as much as I was compelled to, which meant that, when she was in the mood for a special candy bar, she would ask me to go the two doors to the end of the block where, across the street, the small concrete-block grocery store kept a well-stocked sweets counter, and there'd be an extra quarter for me to get myself a special treat.

On the days that the rolling store came down our street – about three times a week – I didn't even have to walk the two doors to get her candy bar because the candy bar came to us.

A rolling store? You may well ask *what* is a rolling store, to which the answer is whatever its operator wants it to be. A few were custom-built, and configured to be much like grocery stores on wheels. Most, however, were makeshift, adapted from used vehicles and kitted out with whatever display equipment the owner could make or scrounge up. Ours was of the latter variety, an old school bus that had been painted avocado green, with no lettering or other identification to mar its pitted surface. To allow the operator greater latitude in how he used the inside and to facilitate the inclusion of as much stock as possible, he had removed all the seats, covered many of the bus's windows, and

installed an array of shelving and bins. His display might have been haphazard in terms of decorative coordination, but it was well thought out. In fact, the man was a genius in retail marketing placement. As you entered the bus, the very first thing you saw was a candy display just at the height of a kid's eye. As you moved further inside, there were sections devoted to fresh produce in season, with a hanging scale, and various kinds of canned goods – soups, vegetables, and a favorite of mine, Beanie Weenies. There were no dairy, meat, or frozen foods available, but that didn't seem to matter to the rolling store's clientele, which was mainly interested in the fresh produce it brought around.

The whole street knew when the rolling store was to arrive, so my grandmother and I would wait on the front porch for it to make its way to our house. Once the bus stopped in front, I was dispatched to find out if the gentleman had anything special that day. My grandmother, being as large as she was, didn't like to make her way down the steps, across the yard, and up into the "store," so if she wanted to examine the produce, I or the store man would bring it to her rocking chair. Only then could a deal be struck.

Afterwards, when she was in a good mood, and if I had not been an aggravation to her, my grandmother would allow me to select something from the wonderful candy assortment on board. Usually, I'd go for a Baby Ruth Bar which was a particular favorite during my ten-to-twelve-year-old period. Other kids favored Butterfingers, Milky Ways, Paydays, and Zero Bars. The first three options I could understand, but Zero Bars were a mystery. To someone who'd grown up on Hershey Bars and homemade fudge, white candy just didn't seem right. Not that dark candies were in this situation necessarily the perfect choice, the problem being the inevitable meltage from their having been carried around in summer in a bus with no air conditioning. I guess maybe the kids who preferred Paydays were on to something.

During the times my grandmother was not in residence with us, at least on the days when the part-time housekeeper wasn't on duty, I was a latchkey kid. While school was in session I had absolute freedom from three in the afternoon to about 6:30. My only duty was to call my mother at work and report in, tell her where I was going to be, and promise to behave.

During most of the summer, on those days when I was unattended, I was free from eight in the morning until 6:30 in the evening. On many of these days I was free to choose my own menu, and I had my strategy down pat. I'd go up to our little local grocery store early in the day and get a quart of chocolate milk and a thin, crusty loaf of locally baked French bread almost two feet long. The proper way to consume this less-than-balanced meal was to return home, eat about a third of the bread, drink about a third of the milk, let them combine inside my stomach and expand into a satisfying lump which would last a few hours of play. Every now and then I would run home and consume another third and so on. This limited menu was strictly my doing. There was always plenty of food to eat, either already prepared or within even a kid's capabilities, but making sandwiches or heating up soup was too time-consuming, given my daily schedule of important kid activities. The only drawback to my French bread-chocolate milk regimen – at least the only one that should be mentioned in an account meant for consumption in polite company – was that my stomach tended to make odd noises!

CHAPTER SIX

ALLEY SCAVENGING OR EARLY RECYCLING

The alleys that divided each block in our neighborhood into two east-west rectangles were not paved, but surfaced in hard gravel. All of the neighborhood lots backed up to an alley, providing a handy place in the inset behind the garage for homeowners to leave not only their metal garbage cans, but also anything else they considered trash, there to wait until, three times a week, city sanitation trucks rumbled up and down, collecting anything they found.

It was in the interim period, between the time of putting out and picking up, that Vernon and I would cruise all the nearby alleyways for anything we might be able to use in our various experiments and construction projects. We'd walk along, kicking at gravel, peering into back yards, some of which were fenced and held dogs. These dogs had become so accustomed to our scrounging routine that they didn't even bother to bark unless Torchy and Smut, two more-or-less free-ranging neighborhood dogs of vaguely beagley background, happened to be tagging along with us.

Save for the carefully landscaped courtyard of the president of the syrup-manufacturing company, my namesake, and the gravel-strewn yard of the mechanically minded neighbor (the wife-avoiding, car-repairing train engineer), all the back yards were much the same: small, tidy, and devoid of personality, patches of well-trimmed grass with a narrow concrete walk that led from back door to garage side door. Given the lack of imagination on show, it was

surprising to see the variety of trash the householders would put out on a regular basis. We'd examine everything with an analytical eye in relation to whatever we were working on at the moment. Certain items, however, remained high on our list at all times: wheels from any source (old baby strollers, lawn mowers, wagons, metal roller skates, scooters, and bicycles); lumber of any sort that could be fashioned into something useful; and anything that looked as if it might be instructive to bash apart and see what was inside.

All of these we viewed as valuable additions to our stockpile. The only recyclable items we used as moneymakers were soft-drink bottles. Most brands had a monetary value from two cents to five cents. These were always gathered on the first alley ride-through. If there were treasures that couldn't be carried on bicycles or dragged behind us, we would return with my red Radio Flyer wagon and haul the treasure to either my yard or Vernon's. Certain items were sure to go to Vernon's because his father had a very complete woodworking shop built onto the family's garage, which was useful for deconstructing or reconstructing our alley finds. These raw materials went into the making of push cars, wooden scooters, tree houses, forts, and, once, a land-locked airplane with fully articulated system of rudder, ailerons and flaps controlled by an iron fireplace poker.

To finance these urban work projects, we used our allowances and whatever we got for the soda bottles we turned in at the neighborhood grocery store and Shepard's Shoe Shop for hard cash. On a good week, we pulled in two or three dollars on the bottles, but usually less. Sometimes there were minor disputes as to whose bottles were whose and how the cash was to be divided. Usually, it was pooled for purchasing items needed to finish a project. One time, for example, we spent some of the pooled funds at the hardware store for steel pipe and pipe caps to make pirate pistols.

The idea for the pistols was an outgrowth of a scavenging find behind a typewriter-repair shop we passed on the way home from a balsa-wood glider purchase at Shepard's, paid for by bottles we'd turned in. To our delighted surprise, this typewriter-repair shop throwaway yielded a handful of ball bearings, probably from defunct office machines of some sort, that had been casually tossed into the alley. Once back to our lair we hammered them to bits and retrieved many beautiful steel balls about ¼ to ½ inch in diameter. Wow, we thought, this would make great shot for some sort of gun. That's how the design of the pirate pistols began. Not going into great detail, let's say they were an effective, muzzle-loading, firecracker-powered brace of pistols which gave us many hours of seaborne make-believe. The amazing thing was that everyone assumed the guns didn't actually work, maybe because we were careful not to shoot them when anyone who could tell us to stop was around. But work they did!

CHAPTER SEVEN

MY FIRST NAKED LADY AND OTHER ROMANTIC ATTACHMENTS

Let me take you back, way back, in my bank of special memories well past the brain's cortex into the cerebellum where, in an alcove sacred to quivering lust, there will always reside an image etched in full color. The subject is a smiling lady of indeterminate age just finishing her shower. She is peering around the shower curtain, immaculate, luxuriant dark hair, mysteriously dry, hanging around her shoulders, her hand modestly holding the curtain so that only one of her wondrous breasts is exposed. Just one breast? No matter, to my ten-year-old eyes, she was a revelation, and a life-long interest was kindled.

I must admit I never owned this treasure. I was, however, allowed to view it for about a minute at the cost of twenty-five cents.

Then the next lucky boy in line paid his quarter and so on and so on until recess was over and the wrinkled and frayed magazine page on which the image lived had to be put away by its owner, a classmate and budding entrepreneur named Roy.

Roy's father had died in the Second World War, and he lived with his mother, stepfather, and younger brother in an area of smaller houses built since the War. He was an all-around cut-up and class bad boy. Well, not really *bad* bad, just bad in the sense of flaunting the rules of the school and society in general, which he did so effectively that he spent a large part of most school days either on his way to the principal's office, waiting outside the principal's office, or in the principal's office. Oddly enough, he and the principal, Miss Dilmore, had what amounted to something of a bond, probably because they'd spent so much time together. Once, when I arrived late and had to deliver a written excuse from my mother to the school office, I found myself an accidental eavesdropper to one of their encounters.

"Oh, Roy," Miss Dilmore said in her firm, pleasant voice, "what am I going to do with you?"

There was a brief pause, as if the question was being seriously considered, then Roy responded sadly, "I really don't know, Miss Dilmore."

There was a longer pause, then Miss Dillmore continued, "You should try to behave better, Roy."

"Yes, Miss Dillmore," Roy agreed.

"Will you at least *try* to behave better, Roy?"

"Yes, Miss Dillmore," Roy said earnestly.

"Ooooh, Roy." The distressed resignation in Miss Dillmore's voice showed she thought the odds of that were slim.

I was still standing at the office counter, waiting to have my excuse stamped to take to the teacher, when Miss Dillmore and Roy appeared. She patted him on the arm, and he gave her a surprisingly nice smile and left. When I went into the hallway to go to class, he was waiting. I thought for a minute that he was going to do something to me for overhearing him in Miss Dillmore's office, but he just grinned and said we might as well walk to class together, which we did in a companionable silence.

To a meek, skinny kid like me Roy was a joy to watch. When he was bored with school – he left. When he was hungry – he ate. When he wanted you out of his way – you moved. He had a reputation as a bully, but he only bullied the other bullies. I never saw him lean on one of us "lesser kids," and he was known to stand up for girls who were being too roughly teased by the meaner boys.

Roy was our source for all sorts of contraband, and his

understanding of the needs of his clientele was unsurpassed. Gum, candy, cigarettes, and naughty comics were his stock in trade, always fresh and in good condition. He was able to keep his classmates supplied with these necessities because he ignored the fact that the store across from the high school around the corner was off limits. He wouldn't bother to hide what he was doing but would walk in, insolently look around, state his requirements, throw the money down on the counter, collect his product, and leave. Given that few of the rest of us had the nerve to patronize the store and so were dependent on him, Roy's prices weren't exorbitant, but volume gave him what had to be a pretty good profit margin because he was self-financed, always paying cash but not collecting from buyers until the moment of delivery. Much as I enjoyed the Mounds Bars Roy sold me, however, it's Miss Shower Curtain for which I remember him best.

Only a year or two later, I somehow "stumbled" across my old man's naughty-photo stash (souvenir of his wartime occupation duties in Europe). These photos, not in the least pornographic, were nonetheless somewhat more risqué than Roy's magazine page, and some of the women in them were better looking. It occurred to me that I could take them to school and maybe trade Roy a glimpse of them for another look at Miss Shower Curtain. Still, the care my father had taken in hiding them showed that my using them for show and tell could result in my being grounded forever. The risk was too great. I regretfully took a last look and replaced them exactly as found. I never saw them again, but I'll admit that the memories of one or two linger in the alcove in my brain sacred to quivering lust, well-placed but definitely behind Miss Shower Curtain. That was obviously a quarter well spent with Roy on that dusty playground during fifth-grade recess.

My becoming interested in the female form led directly to art appreciation. Around the time of the "lady in the shower," I was exposed to a real live beauty and – along with all the other boys in school – became completely infatuated with her.

Her name was Miss Manfred, and she was the art teacher in our grammar school. She was pretty, gentle, artistic, and a recent runner-up state beauty queen. I mean the big one – the Miss America Pageant. Even though she was a runner-up to the state titlist, to us boys and (I believe) girls too, she was a winner.

I slaved away at any task she set before me, trying to gain her admiration and hopefully her personal attention. When she would hover over my desk to admire my latest artistic endeavor, the scent of her perfume would make me giddy. I think that was the main impression she made. I mean, her physical appearance was really something – medium height, slender but shapely, blonde, blue-eyed, a turned-up nose, an extremely fair complexion, and a predilection for wearing well-fitted sweater sets – but that scent was the image, if a scent can have an image, that I always carried away with me as I walked out of art class, on Cloud Nine some days because she'd tacked my latest drawing onto the bulletin board. I never knew the name of her perfume, just that it was spicy and piquant, yet light, definitely not the nose-numbing *White Shoulders* preferred by my mother.

Unfortunately, our boyish hearts – mine and that of all the other young males in our class – were broken when, upon returning from summer break, we learned from Miss Manfred herself that she was to be married very soon and would become *Mrs. Easton*. Mrs. Easton! Ugh. That sounded so official, like she was to be some sort of principal, or old, or mean. Was it possible, we wondered, that Miss Manfred would become the typical slave-driving teacher and art class like all the other classes we dreaded?

A few weeks later, her role having been briefly filled by a substitute teacher, a grumpy man whose scent, as Roy boisterously pointed out was *Eau de Sweat*, Miss Manfred – I mean Mrs. Easton – returned to us, but it was never the same. I think she even smelled different. I know I hated that Mr. Easton for taking my art muse away. The next semester, she was gone. No explanation. Just gone. Yes, gone, but evidently not forgotten.

As for Roy - instinctively insubordinate and entrepreneurial - he remained an inspiration for some time to come.

CHAPTER EIGHT

MY SHOE-SHOP SOURCE

Roy might have been necessary at school, but after school and on weekends, I was an experienced shopper – thanks in part to being a latchkey kid with an allowance I could spend any way I wanted. One of my favorite places for all sorts of things was a shoe shop. Don't be misled by that description, for a shoe shop is not always a shoe shop. Mine – Shepard's - was a varied emporium of kid delights, a mom-and-pop operation located at The Point, a five-way intersection about four blocks from my street, in the heart of an assortment of odds-and-ends businesses. Around The Point, in addition to Shepard's, there were a pharmacy (with a good comic-book rack), a hardware store, a grocery store, a florist, a beauty shop, a wonderful barbeque joint, a tiny, two-chair barber shop, a Texaco filling station, a typewriter-repair shop, and a general-repair shop where we sometimes left a temperamental radio or lamp.

As for Shepard's, they worked on shoes, leather purses, briefcases, and belts. Most of us had at one time or another left things there for our parents, to be tagged, put into one of the numbered bins behind the counter, and collected in a few days with their problem areas repaired and leather gleaming like new. In the section of the shop given over to the leather part of the business, Mr. Shepard worked continuously, sewing new soles to shoe uppers, reattaching high heels, and threading new laces through oxford eyelets with amazing rapidity as he puffed away on his pipe.

Shoe repair, however, was but part of Shepard's business, for – in spite of competition offered by the pharmacy and grocery store – it was the neighborhood source of choice for the most-basic needs of us kids. In a display case up front, they had all sorts of sweet things (including every brand-name candy and gum known to us) and, in an old cooler on a side wall, a decent array of the kinds of beverages kids like; but the mainstays that really drew us in were the more-specialized offerings, in particular pink bubblegum cigars, candy cigarettes, candy buttons, circus peanuts, marshmallow ice-cream cones, wax lips, vampire teeth and little Coca-Cola-shaped wax bottles filled with a mysterious green fluid. This part of the enterprise was under the supervision of Mrs. Shepard, and she was remarkably patient with the indecisiveness that was inevitable when kids were faced with this much choice.

Once we'd selected our sweet of the day, we would gravitate to the third section of Shepard's, which was devoted to a limited selection of toys. There were cast-metal cars and trucks for the boys and movie-star paper-doll books for the girls. The products that Vernon and I bought most often at Shepard's, however, were the balsawood gliders. These fragile flyers lasted for about an hour of hard use, which was certainly their lot with us. They cost only a dime, but we ran through a lot of them, so many in fact that the expense would prompt us – instead of returning our alley-scavenging bottles to the grocery store for hard cash – to bring the empty soda-pop bottles to Shepard's, where the deposit proceeds would return immediately to their cash drawer in payment for our new stash of gliders (unless the money had to go toward a part for one of our alley-scavenging projects). The generally good-natured Shepards did not much like this arrangement, as they had to turn the bottles in to their drink distributor, who was also resistant to deposit refunds, but they would oblige us once a day. The rest of the time, we had to come up with the money

if we wanted anything from Shepard's, gliders or otherwise.

Shepard's had another kind of product that interested me as a budding artist. Next to the toy case was a small display of art supplies. When I was in the mood, I would look over the meager selection of crayons, chalk, paper pads and brushes. I didn't buy anything very often, there being no point in spending my own money on art supplies since my parents considered them an educational expense and so something for which they were almost always willing to pay. Only a genuine art emergency would prompt me to stand before the supply display, inhaling the mixture of aromas – shoe polish, leather, candy, tobacco smoke, and Juicy Fruit gum - debating seriously whether it was really worth it to hand over part of my allowance to buy something that my parents would buy for me if only I was willing to wait a few days until I could get them to the art store. Usually, greed won out, and I'd turn away from the needs of art and back to the contemplation of Shepard's array of wax lips and vampire fangs, which was – even in the opinion of connoisseurs like myself – truly exceptional and certainly more immediately important to a boy than a new box of crayons.

CHAPTER NINE

GOING DOWNTOWN

Downtown was a perfect blending of everything a foot-loose kid could conceive – five-and-dime stores, movies, food, candy, freedom and adventure all packed into about five square blocks. This wonderland, less than three miles from my doorway, was easily reached by bus in about fifteen minutes at a cost of twenty cents.

Saturdays were looked forward to all year around because it was then that – barring parental interference – the kids on my block, at least the boys, made the pilgrimage to this Mecca of amusement. We weren't allowed to go by ourselves, so without much discussion we formed a loose-knit group for the purpose, usually numbering three or four boys all more or less the same age who waited together for the downtown-bound Number 26 bus that stopped at the top of our street. Besides myself, the regulars would include Bobby, who lived across the street, Jerry, from the other end of the block, and sometimes Freddie from the next street over.

These trips began when we were about ten and lasted until we became teenagers and sometimes a little longer. No adult ever accompanied us, but we were definitely not without adult oversight. Bobby's mother was manager of the large lunch counter at the downtown Sears store; and Mrs. Lilmouth, the war widow who lived a couple of houses away, was the secretary to the manager of the State Theater. Both these connections not only made our parents feel better about letting us go downtown on our own, but also provided certain advantages. It was no hardship, for example, that we were required to have lunch with Bobby's mother at Sears (for free). If the feature playing at the State interested us (rarely the case unless there was a John Wayne western or war movie playing), all we had to do to get in for free was to ask the box-office person to call upstairs and get Mrs. Lilmouth's OK. Most of the time our favorite was the smaller Royal Theater which *always* ran cowboy movies. However, we would go to any theater with a Tarzan movie starring Johnny Weismuller, however old the particular feature might be.

The prime objective of these outings wasn't, however, the movies, but the chance to cruise the toy departments of the downtown five-and-dimes: Woolworth's, Newberry's, Grant and Kress. We usually didn't have much money after bus fare and movie tickets, but we enjoyed looking and wishing. It was a good thing to know what was out there when Christmas or birthday-list time came around. In the meantime, one of us would occasionally make a minor purchase, maybe a plastic car or new cap gun.

Our routine on these outings was fairly precise. We'd leave home and board the bus about 10 A.M. to be sure to hit the stores soon after opening. The "shopping" lasted until about 12:30, when we would go to lunch at Sears. While roaming from one store to the other, we would check the movie offerings and times at the seven different theaters then active downtown. This was possible because they were all close together. In just a couple of square blocks we could choose from the State, Ritz, Empire, Star, Royal, Galax (another with mostly Western fare) and the Lyric. The first shows of the day were around 1 P.M. Once the debate on which movie to see was settled, we pooled our remaining cash for refreshments. If there was a double feature that day (hopefully with a Three Stooges epic between features), we were out about 4 to 4:30 P.M.

Afterwards, we would trudge back to the bus stop in

front of Newberry's and – reeking of Orange Crush, popcorn, and Junior Mints and clutching our new, soon-to-be-lost-or-forgotten treasures – would wait for old Number 26 to take us back where we'd started that morning. At home, my parents would ask me if I'd had a good time, and I'd make some casual response that in no way adequately communicated just how much fun I'd had. After all, I'd been downtown.

CHAPTER TEN

THE WEST END WORLD

Even for kids, sometimes movies were just movies. We went, we watched, we walked away, and that was pretty much that. Some movies, however – usually something to do with John Wayne on a horse chasing bad guys or at the controls of a fighter plane shooting down bad guys or on the bridge of a ship pursuing bad guys – would catch our fancy to such an extent that we had to reenact them. If, between us, we boys didn't already have the necessary props on hand, reenactment called for a trip to one or more five-and-dimes, the preferred shopping venue for kid necessities. Of the dime stores, our favorite was Ivey's 5 & 10¢ at West End, an area about a mile and a half from my house, approximately halfway between my neighborhood street and downtown.

Unlike Skidmore's, an old-fashioned West End dime store just up the street with wooden floors and large, dusty window displays, Ivey's was bright with not a dust speck in sight, and organized into merchandise categories indicated by neatly printed signs. Vernon and I came there regularly, hurrying through the front door toward steps at the back that led up to a mezzanine, site of Ivey's hobby section, which stocked a decent assortment of model trains, planes and ships. This was good stuff from the best makers, and priced accordingly. Always frugal in such settings, before committing ourselves we would, over several visits, spend hours upstairs at Ivey's surveying pur-

chasing options (or sometimes getting ideas for projects that we cobbled together ourselves when the going price for store-bought seemed too high).

The shopping excursions for post-movie props rarely involved the relatively pricey mezzanine, for then we were usually after inexpensive stuff, which was found in the general toy section on the main floor. We'd troop past aisles crammed with dishcloths, ponytail holders, shoe laces, grooming aids, cleaning supplies, scissors and sewing supplies, plastic flowers, seasonal ornaments, greeting cards, wrapping paper, picture frames, school supplies and a lot of other boring stuff to get where we were going. Then, past the row of doll sets, toy dishes and cookware sets, metal beach pails, and balloons, and on to board games, boxes of Magic Crystals, tin windup circus wagons, whistles, yo-yos, penny tattoos, tin clickers, dart boards, Buck Rogers space ships, and die-cast sports cars, we'd end up at what we'd come for: the cap guns, popguns, squirt guns, bows and arrows, rubber daggers, play swords, plastic hand grenades, Indian war bonnets, lassos, Western-style toy knives, tin sheriff's badges, peace pipes, plastic Army helmets and any other miscellany we could find to beef up our reenactment capabilities. Then it was back home, where we'd go up and down the alleys, in and out of our individual family back yards, playing at being John Wayne or (if the short straw had been drawn) the villains he always overcame.

Next door to Ivey's was the Allied Drug Store. The main attractions here were the soda fountain and the comic-book racks. I was a devoted reader of the Donald Duck series, especially those featuring Uncle Scrooge and the Beagle Boys. I always relished the idea of swimming in your own pool of money like Uncle Scrooge. In my earlier years, I was also a collector of Little Nancy and Sluggo comics. Even though a lot of my friends didn't like them, something about the series struck me as funny. One way and another, my buddies and I spent a lot of time at Allied.

Joe's Café, on the other hand, across the street and up the way, next door to the West End Theater, was not a kid hangout. The owner didn't encourage young patrons. I guess we didn't spend enough money to take up space in his establishment, the menu for which ran more to adult-type fare: "plate lunches" with meat and two vegetables on a triple-divided plate, with coffee and pie to follow. There wasn't a hot dog or burger in sight - and no ice-cream special-ties - so it was no hardship for us to stay away.

Other establishments in the vicinity that we viewed as pri-marily adult included the beauty parlor and a dentist. Neither of these storefronts held any real interest for us, but we couldn't resist making fun of the name of the dentist – Dr. Delvin Inns, as I recall. I don't know why we thought this name was so hilarious, but we certainly got a lot of snickers out of repeating it as we walked past the dentist's door on our way to Skidmore's, the other area five-and-dime. We rarely found anything we wanted in its dim, dusty precincts, but checked it out every once in a while, just in case.

What made West End a real destination for us, however, wasn't any of the above. The two biggest draws were the local Carnegie Library and the West End Movie Theater, which sat together, divided only by a side street. The library was the place we came to select books for the dreaded book reports required at school. We could have gotten books from the school library, but there were definitely more boy-oriented books at what we always viewed as the *real* library.

The library building itself was interesting. You entered up a wide flight of masonry stairs, through a columned portico and into a dim, sort of spooky interior. The first impression other than the dimness was the smell. A lot of the kids didn't like it. When we walked inside the library building, they'd wrinkle their noses and make a face. Not me. From my first visit, I loved the smell, that fragrance exuded by old books. It was clear that there were a *lot* of them at the West End Library, but I never saw any but those ranged on shelves in the main room because that was where the adventure books were located. In that main room there was a mural that ran high up along the wall above the shelves, a depiction of fairy stories with knights and medieval ladies and strange animals. The lighting was so bad that these images were not so much an actuality, but were rather more of an impression of color and form as the wall reached upwards toward the heavy-corniced ceiling. There were other rooms off this main room, but I never went there. For one thing, the serious-faced librarian – a stickler for rule enforcement – frowned on kids being anywhere but in the main room unless they had a specific reason to go elsewhere; for another, all the kids' books were in the main room, so there was no need to go further.

When you came out of the library and looked across the side street to your left, you faced the long side of the West End Movie Theater, a typical, narrow, late 1920s-style neighborhood theater building. There was no decorative detail either inside or out. It was nothing special at all, except for what transpired every day and twice on Saturday. I knew it well, because it was within easy biking range, a perfect substitute for those Saturdays when for one reason or another our loose-knit group of boys didn't go downtown.

Going to the movies at the West End was a very different proposition than when you went downtown. While downtown movies were new and first run, with big-name movie stars, West End movies were usually anywhere from two to fifteen years old and featured actors that you might – or might not – have heard of before. In fact, nobody who was picky about what he wanted to see went to the West End, for it occupied a very low rung on the movie-distribution ladder. On the other hand, it compensated for its lack of timeliness by sheer quantity. The typical Saturday fare, for example, always from years before, would feature an action flick like *Tarzan and the Mermaids* with a Bowery Boys feature like *Triple Trouble*, with the added bonus of a Three Stooges short title like *Three Pests in a Mess*, with Curly of course. Not to mention a *Merry Melodies* cartoon. No one could say you didn't get a lot for your quarter.

Unfortunately, even a boy as usually oblivious to the finer

nuances of housekeeping as I was couldn't help noticing that the West End was not the best-kept movie house. A horde of rowdy kids descending like locusts every weekend, all stopping at the refreshment stand for sticky, gooey candy bars, greasy popcorn, and sugary soft drinks, could leave a lot of debris and messy traces, and most of it had a tendency to stick around (no pun intended), even after the desultory sweeping out that the part-time usher gave the place once or twice a week. The smell that greeted you when entering the tiny lobby was an almost indescribable mixture of unattended restrooms, stale popcorn, trodden gum, spilled grape soda, and unwashed patrons.

The theater management seemed to consist of an elderly lady whom none of us ever saw outside of the ticket booth, together with an even older gentleman who ran the tiny concession stand and tried to keep some semblance of order. My father, who'd grown up around the corner from the West End, said that when he was young the same old gent was at the theater; they called him "Turk" because of his long, wattly, turkey-like neck. In addition to dispensing sticky treats from the refreshment stand, Turk was also the ticket taker.

This ticket taking resulted in a showdown one day when three of us from my street – me, Jerry and Bobby – presented our tickets for tearing. Jerry and I, just past the magic age of twelve, had virtuously paid our twenty-five-cent admissions, but Bobby – a year older, but smaller than we were, a characteristic he emphasized by employing an extreme slouch at the ticket booth – had gotten away, yet again, with buying a dime ticket. This time, however, Turk's watery eyes took a closer look at him.

"Hey, kid, you can't come in here with a dime ticket anymore. I know you've been coming in here for at least twelve years."

Bobby tried to insist he was only eleven, but to no avail. Turk, wattles quivering, making an unexpectedly stubborn stand, told him go back to the ticket lady and give her fifteen cents more, adding, "I'm telling Mrs. Dunkin to remember you from now on." Which ended Bobby's cheap-ticket scam for good, at least at the West End. (He continued to use it at larger theaters for a couple of years longer.)

After three-and-a-half hours of movie-packed absorption, my stomach queasy from the combination of having eaten too much of Turk's greasy popcorn and smelled too much of the theater's usual ambience, I was totally ready to get back into fresh air. On the way out, we'd look over the lobby posters for next week's offerings like *The Wake of the Red Witch*, a years-old swashbuckling epic with John Wayne, and *Roll on Texas Moon* with my favorite western actor Gabby Hayes. Then, you'd emerge, blinking, into light.

A lot of the devoted kid movie addicts only went to the West End, never missing a Saturday. To them, it was just "the show," as in "Are you going to the show next week?" To us "downtownies," the West End was a fun diversion when we couldn't hit the big movie theaters, not quite up to our usual elevated standard. Even so, we always felt movie-satiated as we walked to the bike racks around the corner from the entrance. The conversation rarely varied.

"Pretty good," one of us would say thoughtfully.

"Yep, pretty good," another would reply.

Then we would pull our bikes out of the rack beside the theater to head downhill toward the neighborhood, yelling out funny things to each other as we coasted toward home.

CHAPTER ELEVEN

THE TWENTY-MULE SUMMER

Not everything I wanted could be had in local stores. There were, for example, those ads in the back pages of magazines aimed at kids wanting to collect stamps. I began to notice them when I was ten or eleven, and who could blame me for thinking that what these little classifieds offered represented a wise investment decision? I mean they would send the astute buyer an improbably large number of "international" stamps for a dime or a quarter or, if you were a really big spender, a dollar. I sent away my dime with high hopes. In due course, the stamps arrived. When I dumped them out of the glassine envelope into which they'd been crammed for shipment, I saw two things: there were a lot of them; and most were from countries I'd never heard of. My enthusiasm was pretty much extinguished after I looked at the catalog that accompanied the colorfully obscure bits of paper and realized that this first order was the last time that anything about stamp collecting would be cheap.

While disappointing, this didn't put me off the concept of ordering from afar. All I needed was for the right opportunity to appear, which it did in the form of the Old Ranger who was the host of the dramatic western show *Death Valley Days*, a radio favorite that had made it to TV by the summer I was twelve. We'd had our TV for less than a year, and I was still capable of sitting in riveted silence before its flickering black-and-white screen for hour after hour. One of my favorite parts of *Death Valley Days*, oddly enough, wasn't the program per se, but the commercial. The sponsor was a cleaning product named Twenty Mule Team Borax, and the sales message prominently featured the image of twenty mules industriously hauling borax from the mines, gamely setting forth across an endless stretch of desert. That visual always fascinated me. By now an experienced Lionel-train wrangler, I was always looking for something new to add to my layout, so when the Old Ranger himself offered me the chance to send away my money and proof of purchase to become the proud owner of a model of the Twenty Mule Team and their cargo, I couldn't address that envelope fast enough. Unfortunately, in my eagerness to find an envelope, I evidently left the room before the Old Ranger added a casual postscript that warned viewers to "allow four to six weeks for delivery."

Subsequent shows made the time issue clearer to me, but I couldn't quite believe they meant it because to a kid four to six weeks is half a lifetime, and who'd want to wait *that* long? So, after a couple of days, I eagerly watched for every mail delivery.

My grandmother had just arrived for her annual routine of summertime kid watching. Watching was all she could do since she was – as they say – stone deaf. Her deafness – which was of a type beyond the hearing-aid technology of the time – was not as much of a handicap as you may imagine. If you were face to face with her, she could read your lips and sometimes, I think, even your mind. This

time, her deafness served her well because she didn't have to listen to me gripe about how long it was taking for my Twenty Mule Team package to arrive.

After a couple of weeks, I began to realize that they had meant four to six weeks, and went back to my favorite pastime, the operation of the Lionel O-gauge railroad layout then residing in the sunroom of our house. You had to hand it to my parents. Most of my friends who had anything similar had to keep it in the garage or in boxes, to be brought out as wanted, but my parents had given over the pretty sunroom adjoining the living room to not only all the Lionel paraphernalia but also to a four-by-eight table full of tooting, clattering, flashing, and (in my opinion, but possibly not theirs) all-around wondrous railroadiana. I pretty much had it all. Besides the roaring trains and some bits of scenery, my layout conained a variety of accessories: an automatic-crossing watchman with a bright red lantern; a flashing red-and-green rotary beacon tower; an operating, bubbling oil derrick; and cars that unloaded milk cans and logs. Yep, I pretty much had that table full. Even so, I could see how I'd use the Twenty Mule Team when it arrived. That team of mules and the three wagons could be approaching the train where a hopper car partly filled with borax would already be waiting.

If anything, as I worked on the layout, my anticipation increased. Weeks crawled by. The summer was beginning to disappear at an alarming rate. My grandmother's patience was also wearing away. I literally bounced up and down in my anticipation. Every day I would wait for the postman to come – nothing. August arrived and still no mules. My belief in American business weakened by the hour.

Still, kids are nothing if not resilient, and while I was eating breakfast one hot early-August day, I found myself tempted by another mail-order offer, this one displayed on my Rice Krispies box. I could be the proud owner of a set of three Snap, Crackle and Pop hand puppets. I had a long-standing interest in puppets – only increased by hours and hours of the *Howdy Doody Show*, which was full of live and manipulated characters. For a moment, I forgot the agony of the Twenty Mule Team waiting game. Money must be pro-cured, the box top had to be ripped off and mailed at once. Announc-ing this to my grandmother brought an unexpected reaction. STONEWALLED. She said no. No money, no envelope, no stamp, and no more talk of mail order. It took a couple of hours of concen-trated sulking on my part before she relented in part. I could order Snap, Crackle and Pop *after* the Twenty Mule Team was delivered, if – as she put it – that ever happened.

Eventually, sometime in late August, the great moment arrived in the form of a rather small box with my name on it and the unmistakable Twenty Mule Team corporate logo in the return address. I was puzzled. Surely a parcel able to hold twenty mules and

three wagons would be long and heavy? Still, it was with great eagerness that I ripped open the box and inspected the contents as I laid
them out on the breakfast-room table. It was a kit! I had to put it
together. On TV two-and-a-half months before, in its sandy desert
environment, it had been shown whole, complete, ready to display.
Now I was confronted with a pile of blue and brown plastic parts.
The blue parts belonged to the wagons. The brown parts were the
mules, divided into four clear plastic bags of five mules each. Each of
the four bags of mules had a different pose: some heads up, some
heads down, and some with different leg positions. There were also
lots of tiny bits of thin plastic harness and a spool of black thread.

I was still sorting through it when my father came in. I whined
to him about my disappointment in finding that I had to put all this
together before I could do anything with it. He looked over the blue-and-
brown mess covering half of the table and told me to put it back in the box
and take it to the workbench in the garage. There, we stood and looked
at it thoughtfully. At the age of twelve, I was no stranger to assembling
plastic kits, but this was daunting. My father suggested we glue the mules
and wagons to a wooden base. So began the agony of assembling twenty
mules (I didn't mention before that each mule came in two pieces) and
three wagons on a thirty-six-inch long 1x4" wood base.

The real test of my modeling skills came with applying the
harness and black-thread reins through a zillion little needle-sized holes.
Once all the bits were glued down to the base, it was time to introduce
this treasure to the railroad room. If before I had been surprised at how
small the disassembled kit seemed, now I was horrified at how big the
assembled version had suddenly become. DAMN! It was too big to fit
anywhere on the train table. Discouraged, but wiser, I took the team to
my bedroom and found a resting place on a shelf above my bed where
its impressive length gathered dust for a couple of years before being
packed away.

I never ordered the hand puppets. My direct-response mail-
order career was over. If I couldn't see an item in front of me and hold it
in my hands, I had no interest in buying it, or at least not enough to go
through *that* again .

CHAPTER TWELVE

POLIO PLUNGE

Let me explain this title as soon as possible. This was our neighborhood's nickname for the local swimming pool located in nearby Wood Park, the closest public pool for most of us kids. During the early 1950s, before the development of the Salk vaccine, polio was a much-feared and widespread affliction considered a particular hazard for children. Many thought that the polio virus could be contracted in swimming pools. Obviously, my parents and the others in our area didn't subscribe to this belief since we all practically lived in Wood Park and other pools around the city during warm weather. My grandmother was more cautious, but usually gave in.

As far as I know, no one ever "caught" polio swimming at Wood Park, but kids being kids, we gave the pool this nickname just like we nicknamed anything else we wanted to make fun of. I don't know whether there were polio germs in the Wood Park pool; however, knowing the habits of some of my buddies, there were plenty of other gruesome things in there. I'm sure it had its quotient of urine, Coca-Cola, sweat, and bits of gum and candy – as well as anything else it occurred to the more lawless among us to toss or release into the murky water. We always said you should swim the breast stroke so your hands would sweep the floating debris to the side.

Our usual mode of transportation to the pool was by bike. Sometime we doubled up two to a bike so we didn't have to be as concerned about thieves, our theory being the fewer the bikes, the less the worry. Even so, as a protective measure, we would usually chain the bike to the wire fence next to the pool so we could keep a close eye on it.

The smell of the boys' locker room was a living organism in gaseous form, being made up mainly of sour towels, wet bathing suits, chlorine, mold and faulty plumbing. Quite a heady stew. Once you had changed, put your clothes in a numbered basket and turned it over to the poor soul who had to stay in that odor all day, you received a quarter-sized metal tag with your basket number on it, which you'd stick into the small pocket just inside the elastic band of your trunks. Then you'd run to the shower room (the rules stated that everyone must shower before the entering the pool), where you ducked under an ice-cold spray. Only then could you go through the door to the pool area.

There was no organized swimming program offered at the Wood Park pool. We just splashed around and had fun. We made the return trip home with bathing suits hung on the handlebar of the

bike, and the warm breeze felt good to our waterlogged, chlorined and pruney bodies after three or four hours in the pool.

As we grew older, we preferred to make the long pilgrimage to the Cascade pool on the other side of town, just too far for reasonable biking. Sometimes we cajoled parents to drive us there and return for us at a set time. This made for an easier ride to the pool, but had a distinct disadvantage for us kids because it meant we had to keep an eye on the time so we wouldn't get fussed at for keeping the adults waiting when they came to collect us. To keep our options open, our preferred method of getting to the Cascade pool was by bus. It was about a forty-five minute trip with one transfer downtown, but we were free to set our own time for arrival and departure.

The reason we were willing to endure this much-longer trek had to do with the facilities offered at Cascade. First, it was much larger, easily two to three times the size of the Wood Park pool. Second, there was a multi-level diving tower which gave us a venue for stupid jumps and dives. Also, there was a more-daring clientele in this part of town. For instance, some of the older boys would tell girls to watch the entrance to the men's locker rooms, then they would go in and strip and jump into the doorway and flash the usually giggling girls. I guess they hoped the girls would reciprocate. If they did, I never saw it. The crowd at Wood Park would never even have thought of this game. I guess we were too young or too naïve.

The nicest pool complex was the Hollywood Country Club, on the south side of town, favored by the elite. As I recall, it was another large pool and very nice, with Spanish Colonial architecture – lots of tile decoration and archways. Those of us in the know, however, tended to avoid Hollywood unless forced to go there for birthday swim parties, because they had *rules,* which they actually enforced. In fact, I can remember being taken there only once.

There were other non-pool swimming venues around the county area for those whose parents would let them go to places that didn't always have lifeguards – lakes or in some cases flooded quarries. The one my parents preferred was a quarry called Holiday Shores that we started going to when I was very young. There was a manmade sand beach, picnic tables and shelters and a big, spooky water slide which took a large amount of nine-year-old nerve to climb all the way to the top, look way down to the lake, and then launch oneself with stomach-churning finality. When I was older, of course, I could do this so casually that anyone around would watch in awe (at least this was what I thought).

Save for the straight-laced Hollywood, these swimming places in all their guises were fun, with the added benefit that, given the gallons of pool, quarry and lake water I must have swilled over the years, by the time I was twelve I had almost certainly built up immunity to just about any disease likely to come my way!

CHAPTER THIRTEEN

NEAR-DISASTER ON THE TRAILWAYS BUS

There were many things dear to a twelve-year-old boy in the 1950s – his bike, his allowance, his favorite ice cream, his Red Ryder BB gun, and his explosives. By explosives, I mean fireworks of all kinds, but especially the loud, powerful, and destructive variety. These included TNT Bombs, Cherry Bombs, MD80s, and some of the more-explosive Bottle Rockets. Of course, there were always needs for the smaller Zebra firecrackers for less-powerful applications, such as our pirate pistols.

The logistical problem in obtaining these necessities of life derived from the fact that they were locally illegal at that time. Luckily for me, my summer visits to my grandparents in an adjoining state with a more-advanced code of jurisprudence gave me access to these weapons of mass destruction. It became well known in my circle of friends that I could fulfill their needs of this sort, however specific and otherwise forbidden. My closest ally and long-time collaborator Vernon would be first to place his yearly order. Vernon, like me an indulged only child, always had money for whatever he wanted. Other orders would follow until I had quite a list of requests.

This illicit traffic went on for about three years. The first two I was driven to and from my grandparents' home by my parents. This made it easy to bring back any amount of loot. I just filled a box with my orders and stashed it in the Buick's trunk (there was enough room in there for a small

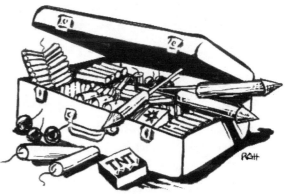

party, much less an extra box or two). The third year, however, my cousin Patrick and I were to be sent on our visit via bus. This began to worry me somewhat in relation to the problem of how to get back home with my consignment of explosives, a venture in which quite a few industrious boys had invested hard-won money. All in all, I had orders amounting to about thirty-five dollars, quite a lot of firepower. Vernon alone was into the game for fifteen dollars worth of goods, and you didn't want to get on his bad side. After some thought, I finally hit on a scheme that promised to work. I would figure out a way to carry two suitcases with me, maybe split my clothes between the two on the way over, and then return with clothes in one and product in the other. Yeah, I thought with satisfaction. That should do it.

My mother thought it odd that I wanted two cases, but decided it wasn't worth the battle and let me carry both, half-filled. The departure day arrived. We met my cousin and aunt at the Trailways bus terminal downtown, where we were put in charge of the bus driver. He was told our destination and that we would be met. Much to my mother and aunt's consternation, he said that this trip we would have to change buses in the first town across the state line, but not on the return. Only after he swore that he would see us safely on the other bus with exact instructions to the next driver, would our anxious mothers allow us to board.

The driver seated us in the front two seats to the right of the entrance door and directly next to him. He obviously didn't intend to let us out of his sight for the next four-and-one-half hours. That was OK with us. These were wonderful seats, right up in the windshield, providing a perfect view of the road. We safely made the trip, including the transfer. Our grandfather met us, and we began our two weeks of freedom.

After a couple of days, I thought I had better get to Chenoweth's, the little family-run general store, to procure my fireworks load before the stock was depleted by the upcoming Fourth of July rush. Chenoweth's carried an odd mixture of merchandise. A long, dark, fragrant interior was divided into various sections of commerce. There were fresh vegetables, general groceries, cold-drink boxes (not coolers, but boxes filled with ice), tobacco goods, candy displays, the ever-popular chips and pork rinds, and – last but not least – the fireworks section. Knowing their clientele, they put the Cherry Bombs next to the Baby Ruths and Butterfingers. The weight of my customers' money in my pocket, I strolled casually up and down the counter displaying the fireworks, firming up my knowledge of what was there compared with what I had on order, and began to fill the list of requests I'd been given. Not wanting to show my hand to Mrs. Chenoweth too soon, I only bought about half of my stock on the first visit, along with an assortment of candy. I finished the order a few days later and began packing the second suitcase with my volatile load. Between the orders I'd filled and my own purchases, I had about forty-five dollars worth of assorted fireworks. I was pleased with what I'd been able to buy, but not so happy when I discovered that all these colorful boxes were not going to fit into one suitcase. The leftovers I had to stuff into the other suitcase with my jeans.

On the day when my cousin and I were to return home, our uncle took us to the bus depot. I watched with trepidation as the station attendant threw my suitcases into the luggage bay in the side of the bus. I couldn't see how anything could set the fireworks off, but I also couldn't help wondering if such rough handling could cause some sort of spark. Patrick, who knew what was in the suitcase, just laughed as I jumped when it hit the side of the luggage bay with a loud thump. I was tempted to say something to him, but – cousin or not – he was unpredictable. I was already regretting telling him about what I was carrying. I was afraid for a minute that he was going to tell on me, but the moment passed and our uncle told us goodbye as soon as the Trailways driver arrived.

The driver was the same man who'd promised to watch over us. He greeted us genially and once more directed us to the front seats. Everything proceeded uneventfully for about three hours. Then the driver announced that he smelled something odd and was going to pull over and check the engine compartment in the rear. I watched him downshift, my heart heavy, petrified with guilt and fear.

What if my explosive-stuffed suitcase was smoldering down in the luggage bay? What if it was about to blow up? The driver pulled the bus into the parking area of a small gas station / store. The manager peered out of the door at this unusual sight, looking hopeful. I guess he thought the bus needed fuel, and lots of it, or at least that the passengers were stopping for a soda break. If so, he was at least partly right. There would be no fuel sold, but the driver did announce to the passengers that they could get out for a stretch and get a snack if they wanted.

As for Patrick and me, we got out too, but stayed near the bus as the driver eased open the engine compartment and began to poke around. I moved closer to the luggage bay, sniffing for signs of smoldering firecrackers. Thankfully, all I smelled was diesel fumes from the rear of the bus. The driver went into the building through the milling crowd of passengers. He soon came out with the owner and some cans of oil and a large funnel. The driver had evidently located the source of the alarming odor, and it didn't have anything to do with me!

As the driver and service-station operator began poking around in the engine compartment, Patrick and I decided we were safe. With a great feeling of relief, we went into the store for some much-needed refreshment. Nothing makes a boy hungrier than guilt-tinged alarm, and a couple of RC Colas and some chips put us in a calmer frame of mind.

Everyone soon re-entered the bus and left a happier store proprietor in our wake. The remainder of the journey went by without any other alarms. I even dozed off over my Scrooge McDuck comic book. Once again back home, I distributed my illegal cargo into eager hands. (The reasonable profit I made on the transactions went into my model-train fund.) Trailways had survived a near miss that day, and so had I.

CHAPTER FOURTEEN

SURVIVING IN THE WILD

My Scouting career had begun early. I joined in 1951, at age eleven, and never regretted it because Scouting was fun, especially the first big regional campout. During the daytime we did all the usual stuff with wood lore, which was interesting. My favorite thing at that first campout, however, was the astronomy lesson. It was a dark, starlit late-summer night. About thirty of us were lying on our backs, gazing upwards as our instructor, standing in the middle of the group, beamed a powerful flashlight into the almost-black sky. He traced the various constellations with the light beam, and related the fables and legends associated with the dippers, archers, bulls, twins, and all their kin. It was like magic except that it was real, and I could hardly go to sleep that night.

Scouting was educational in many ways. We learned about trail cooking and archery from the father of one of the boys, Mr. Erick, who was a champion archer, the winner of many statewide tournaments. He possessed other talents as well, perhaps the most impressive being his ability to cook a one-skillet meal while hunkered down by a tiny rock-rimmed fire. What set him apart from others who could do the same was that his looked "ready for its  close-up," capable of being photographed for inclusion in a slick food magazine. We would stand around in awe as he fried bacon, then a perfect egg, even as bread was being toasted on a stick next to his frying pan. It was an amazing demonstration. When he finished, he sat back on the ground and ate his beautiful, hot breakfast as we wandered back to our communal fire to burn some beans and mis-scramble eggs on a blazing inferno of a fire. We hadn't learned much from Mr. Erick's demo. We always thought the more fire the better.

Complicating our cooking efforts was the fact that there were those among us who didn't understand the "mine-thine" concept. Every group of boys has its resident bully, and ours was a kid named Jerry (not my neighbor, another Jerry), big for his age, spoiled rotten, and mean. We usually just put up with his bad behavior, partly because his size made him difficult to take on, but mostly because, if you did, his mother – a local political power – would show up afterwards and demand that the one who'd attacked her innocent son be disciplined. Which was why we were so tickled when, for once, Jerry's greed did him in. It was a fall campout. My neighbor Billy had brought along some canned biscuits and was baking six of them in a reflector oven about a foot-and-a-half from a small but hot pine-knot fire. The principle was that the shiny metal box's shelf reflected the fire's heat back onto the biscuits. It actually worked pretty well, but you had to give it time. As Billy's biscuits began to cook, they gave off a wonderful aroma in the frosty air. A small group of hungry boys gathered around, sniffing and watching the biscuits turn golden brown. Suddenly, Jerry pushed his way to the front of the group, reached down, grabbed two of the six biscuits, and – over Billy's protests – crammed the first biscuit into his mouth. His eyes popped open, his mouth popped open. Out came a molten mess of half-raw, hot, gooey dough. We all laughed as he spit out the remnant and threw the other biscuit at Billy before stomping away. Billy laughed too, but was careful to let the other biscuits bake until they were a very dark brown before he took them up for buttering.

Food was always important to a bunch of growing boys, who stayed perpetually hungry no matter how much they'd eaten or how recently. At the annual statewide campout in the summer we ate in a big canvas-topped mess hall. As we came bursting in for lunch, we saw that each table was set up with a *large* jar of peanut butter, knives, and two king-sized loaves of bread slit open halfway, standing on end. This, it turned out, was our appetizer, intended to keep us occupied until each table's number was called and its occupants could enter the chow line. Boy, could we pack away some food!

At that same campout, there was a nighttime initiation ceremony for the Order of the Arrow, which was the equivalent of a national honor society for the Boy Scouts. Its membership consisted of an elite group of gung-ho Senior Scouts and Camp Councilors that I never had any idea of aspiring to. Even so, I had to admit that they put on a spectacular show for us.

The setting was on the edge of a large lake with a small island about two hundred yards from shore. The ceremony started after dark about 9:30. The audience gathered on the shore, sat in the grass and waited. Soon we could hear distant drums thumping over the water. Finally, we could see a flicker of torchlight out on the water, moving slowly toward the island, and the drumming continued. Now we could see two canoes draw up to the near side of the island. Four Indians (Camp Councilors) dismounted with the torch. They then began to chant with the drums. Suddenly they stopped, as did the drums. The torch was extinguished. Total darkness. Total silence. Then a flaming arrow flew out over the startled audience and landed on the island.

For a second or two we just saw sparks, then suddenly the drums began again and a huge fire blazed up on the island, illuminating the "Indians," who – after re-lighting the torch – began to chant again. Soon they moved back to the canoes. Re-launching them, they came ashore with the torch. Silently, they walked among us, looking for someone. They selected two boys (the initiates) and took them back to the fire on the island. Then, after more chanting and dancing about, the group disappeared into the darkness on the island.

That was it. Even the cynics among us were moved to silence. It had been quite a show. Dazed by the lateness of the hour, we trudged back to our tents fully impressed with what we'd just seen. The guy next to me put into words what a lot of us were thinking.

"What does it take to get into that outfit anyway?"

But we all knew the question was rhetorical. We were in Scouting for the fun of it not the glory, and it was unlikely that any flaming arrows would fly for us.

CHAPTER FIFTEEN

TRICK OR TREAT

The return to school in the fall was not something any of us kids looked forward to, for it meant the end of freedom for another nine months. There would be no more trips to the swimming pool, no more campouts, no more lazy days spent watching TV, no more anything that we considered fun. In their place would be endless hours in classrooms, fire drills, and homework. The one bright spot as we trudged back to the large brick building that housed our grade school, new book bags in hand, was Halloween, our second-favorite holiday. This hung on the horizon like a bright spot in a suddenly dull world.

Not of all of us prioritized the holiday the same, of course. There were a lot of Halloween parties in our area, and you'd always get invited to at least one. I went to a couple and was shocked to discover that some of the kids used them as a substitute for trick-or-treating. They just went to the party and ate cupcakes covered with bright orange frosting, listened to ghost stories, played spin-the-bottle or some other stupid game while the party-giver's parents looked on, and went home.

For Vernon and me, this didn't cut it. You had to trick-or-treat, or it wasn't Halloween, not really. Of course, even those kids who agreed with us didn't always give the occasion proper respect. Some of them even wore generic costumes. They'd settle for a ghost mask or a monster mask or a witch mask and let their mothers drape them in an old sheet. Vernon and I were not those kids. We put a lot of thought into Halloween, because in our opinion the only way to do it properly

was to be a genuine character. Of course, it was even better when you came up with a way to be *two* genuine characters, which was the strategy that Vernon and I employed to increase our haul.

The process was simple enough. We went out with at least two masks each, wearing a body costume that could work with any of the identities, even going so far as to practice different voices and ways of walking to differentiate our various disguises. When a particularly good treat was handed out, we would make a mental note of the house and return later, having switched masks and demeanors, to collect another round. (I remember one year a neighbor a block over was handing out full-size Mounds bars – I think we hit him at least three times.) Our repeat strategy worked flawlessly most of the time; however, some householders would notice that our basic costumes looked familiar and would question us or turn us away. One year we decided to defeat even their suspicions by having not only dual masks, but also some changeable costume items – different hats, capes, and scarves to produce completely new looks in a matter of minutes. It worked – we were able to hit some houses three or four times without so much as a questioning glance from the person handing out the treats.

I won't pretend that I'd always been this creative. In earlier years, I was like all the other normal little kids on the block with their store-bought outfits: the Cowboy; the Indian; the Princess; the Pirate; and so on. These were the standard dime-store issue, but at about age eleven, I began to want to do custom looks. I guess it was the fledgling art director kicking in. Anyway, I began to search out and invest in better masks and accessories. I would have my mother sew bits of black cloth onto an old discarded coat to make it more like my idea of what a vampire or zombie would wear, concepts formed in dark neighborhood theaters on Saturday afternoons watching *Abbott and Costello Meet the Wolfman* and other movies of this type. It seemed to me that this attention to detail gave the whole trick-or-treating exercise more point. Vernon, always ready to up the ante, went along with this more-ambitious scheme of disguise, driving his mother crazy with his increasingly complex costuming demands.

One of these years, I was fortunate to acquire a particularly gross full-head mask of a slimy green and gray, rotting Zombie, which I wore with a dirty-gray shroud-like costume. At most doorways, I was greeted with comments like, "Hey, honey, come look at this kid – he's the best I've seen tonight." Which was exactly the reaction I was looking for. There was, however, a drawback to this look. If a little kid happened to open the door, the result could be more spectacular than I'd hoped for. One five-year-old charged with handing out the treats took one look at me, dropped the plastic pumpkin full of candy he was holding, and fled screaming into the living room. His mother came to the door to see what had set her little darling off. Seeing me stooped over and grunting, swinging my arms like a zombie, she began to lecture me on Halloween manners and how I should be ashamed of myself for scaring her kid. I waited until she sputtered to a stop and then said, "Trick or treat." She slammed the door in my ugly face.

Lucky for her, I was not with Vernon, who was working the other side of the street. If he'd had to listen to her whining, there would have been a trick played. I'll admit I considered it myself, but I wasn't armed with anything but candy and I wasn't going to waste any of that on these ingrates. I mean, come on, it's Halloween. You're supposed to have the crap scared out of you, right?

CHAPTER SIXTEEN

THE BOOK-REPORT SCAM

I have always been an artist.

There are photos of a young me proudly standing over a chalk drawing of a large truck rendered on the always-available canvas of the concrete sidewalk in front of our house. I look to be maybe four years old.

All my school books were filled with drawings, doodles, symbols and all manner of scribbling. My right hand had a reckless mind of its own. If I had a pencil, pen, crayon, or chalk at hand, I would compulsively draw, almost without thinking.

It was puzzling to me when, in first grade, the teacher gave us a test to determine if we could (a) read the names of colors, (b) select that color crayon, and (c) fill in the appropriate color in a mimeographed page printed with four circles.

Was it a joke? I dutifully did as I was told, thinking that, surely, there was a catch. I had been coloring everything that got in my way for at least four years, maybe more. I was very experienced in coloring within the lines. This was stupid!

Art might come naturally to me; English, however, was more of a challenge. Book reports, in particular, were absolute torment. We had to read books from approved lists and once a week pick one to write a report on. Unlike art, report writing did *not* come naturally to me. After some flailing away, however, I developed a strategy. From that time forward, my reports would consist of three components. One – read the book or try to fake it by reading the book jacket if it had one, and then read the first, middle and last chapters. Two – try to come up with some sort of story line from these endeavors. Three – try to write the resulting literary masterpiece according to the strict rules of penmanship: Keep neat margins on both sides of the paper, write neatly in ink, spell correctly, and don't turn in a blotchy or smudgy paper.

We even had a roving penmanship teacher, Miss Poore, who would come to our school periodically and make a valiant effort to teach us the proper Spenserian script methods. Poor woman, her name was so apt. What a thankless task she had.

In any event, my book-report strategy got me through sixth grade, usually resulting in Bs and Cs (mostly Cs). It was in seventh grade that I had the great epiphany that led to a new and improved book-report era, triggered by my discovery of the adventure writer Richard Haliburton.

Haliburton was a genuinely larger-than-life character, who had ensured his street cred with boys by – among other things – retracing Ulysses' path in *The Odyssey*, swimming the Panama Canal,

tracking on foot Cortez's conquest of Mexico, and then disappearing at age thirty-nine, mid-ocean, while attempting to sail a Chinese junk from Hong Kong to San Francisco. What a guy! Along the way, he managed to churn out books about his exploits. They were hugely popular, especially his first, *The Royal Road to Romance*, a cross between a National Geographic documentary and pages from Indy Jones' diary.

Anyway, it was one of Haliburton's books – I can't remember which – that inspired my book-report scam. Well, not exactly a scam, but let's just say a way to level the playing field with my classmates, some of whom had the unfair advantage of being able to punctuate and spell. Most kids didn't put real covers on their book reports, just wrote the title. I'd done it that way myself. This time, taking a clue from the book's coverage of exotic locales, I designed a gaudy, full-color cover showing a silver 1930s airplane circling around a volcano in full eruption. This masterpiece was rendered in the medium of colored pencils, and then pasted onto a heavyweight black paper, which was folded over to form the report cover. I then stapled my meager three report pages inside. I managed three pages only because of generous margins all around, but at least this time I had actually read the book. The result was a B+ grade, and the report was thumbtacked to the bulletin board.

A winning strategy had been born! From then on, I chose books that would inspire full-color covers. Titles like *Treasure Island*, *Tom Sawyer*, and other adventure-laden epics tweaked my artistic imagination and kept me ahead of most of my competition. Never again was I to see a "C". From then on, all the way, it was "Bs" and even the occasional "A".

And so I made a wonderful and empowering discovery: a picture *is* worth a thousand words.

CHAPTER SEVENTEEN

CHARLIE AND THE CHOCOLATE SOLDIERS

Scouting went on year-round. Most Friday evenings, winter, summer, spring and fall, our troop met at 6:30 in one of the assembly rooms at The Point Baptist Church. I'd come in from school, mess around a little bit, then put on my Scout uniform – or at least my uniform shirt, kerchief and cap, as I usually wore jeans instead of my uniform pants. Friday was payday. My parents would hand over my allowance for the week (usually $2.50) and tell me to be careful, then I'd jump on my bike and head for The Point with plenty of time to spare.

The time was needed because my immediate goal was Charlie's Barbecue, which lay conveniently on the way from my house to the location of the Scout meeting. To understand the significance of Charlie's for me, you have to have a little background on my previously unsatisfactory relationship with food.

First of all, there was the fact that – for a variety of reasons – everything cooked at our house was over-processed, my mother's philosophy being that if you could recognize it, it wasn't done.

Then there were the school lunches, the other primary source of sustenance in my life. Our school, like all grade schools in the city, had a lunchroom, a large, cavernous room on the first floor with cafeteria-style food service on one side and rows of wooden tables, each with six chairs, filling up the rest of the room. Each class was assigned a time to go to lunch, and we'd troop dutifully downstairs or up the hall, through the double doors, and get in the lunch line.

The food on offer varied widely as to its taste appeal. The salmon patties were okay, the banana salad and tomato salad pretty good if you got them early in the week, and the chocolate-frosted sheet cake ditto. The fruit cocktail was canned and usually opened just beforehand, so if you liked the taste of canned fruit cocktail (which I did at the time), it was OK. The ice-cream sandwiches, cups, and Popsicles were about what you'd expect (except for the time a girl at the next table found a fly frozen between the chocolate coating and vanilla body of her Popsicle and let out a squeal that's probably still bouncing around those grimly green walls).

As for the rest, it was pretty dismal. The veggies were cooked according to my mother's doneness standard; the meats were limp and greasy. The wax paper that wrapped the sandwiches was soaked through with oil from the peanut butter or mayonnaise that formed the main ingredient of the sandwiches. When you unwrapped the wax paper, the bread crusts were hard and the fillings watery. As for the salads, the Jell-O was rubbery and almost crusty on all sides, the lettuce always limp and often speckled with brown, and - by Wednesday - the mayonnaise that served as both garnish and binder had a film over it. The desserts were a mixed bag, depending on the day of the week and your luck. The cake that had started out so tastily on Monday in the form of a fresh sheet with fresh frosting that the dessert-and-drink lady sliced to order gradually deteriorated by Friday into stale crumbs mixed up with whipped cream and canned nut syrup, after going through assorted chunkings, choppings, and combinations along the way.

About the only time I had what even as a kid I considered good food was when I visited my grandparents in the summer, where I enjoyed simple but attractive and properly prepared food of the country-fried steak / creamed potatoes / sliced tomatoes sort that my grandfather preferred.

Which takes me back to Friday Scout nights and Charlie's Barbecue at The Point. This little joint, a neighborhood gastronomic destination, was actually run by Charlie (whose last name I never knew) in a tiny, narrow, brick building next to the pharmacy and across the street from the local Texaco gas station. Charlie's was known primarily for its barbecue, but it had a pretty varied menu. There were hot dogs, hamburgers, cheeseburgers, grilled cheese sandwiches, and two or three dubious-looking pies under grease-tinged plastic covers.

To me, it was the equivalent of heaven. Not only did I get to choose exactly what I wanted from the menu, but my selection would arrive in prime condition, freshly prepared and hot or cold as indicated by the description. What I wanted was my weekly infusion of custom-ordered grease and sugar, and it was with a light heart and taste buds already beginning to tingle that I'd lean my bike against the light pole outside and go into the steamy little joint.

Architecturally, Charlie's was an efficient design for its purpose. Being very narrow and deep, it had a front and rear entrance aligned along a straight, tight corridor. On the left, as you entered the front, was the main serving counter, with about eight revolving stools. Opposite were four tiny square tables, each with two attached stools. Near the front, adjacent to where Charlie worked, was the cash register. This arrangement didn't leave much room for the cooking or the cook. This was not good planning, for Charlie – owner, cashier and chef – was big. I could never figure out how he squeezed himself between the counter and the grill. When he was cooking, carrying on two or three conversations with patrons, his ample, apron-covered belly spread over part of the grill.

When he somehow managed to rotate to the counter to serve, his smoldering, greasy apron overlapped the moist Formica surface by about six inches. As for when he turned toward the wood-fired barbecue pit – which was positioned on the wall between the ends of the grill and the serving counter – you didn't want to watch for fear that, this time, the apron would go up in smoke. His apron was a culinary art object. Grease, food stains, burns, and handprints made up a design that Salvador Dali would have envied.

I went to this emporium of good eats often enough that Charlie remembered my standing order of cheeseburger and a Chocolate Soldier. (In case you have never heard of a Chocolate Soldier, it was a tall glass bottle of chocolate-flavored liquid, something like a Yoo-Hoo.) In spite of my regular patronage, I was a kid; and, as such, was relegated to one of the little tables on the right wall. The counter seats were reserved by tacit agreement for the grownups who made up Charlie's regular clientele (some of them seemed to eat all their meals there). When my order was ready, I was summoned to approach the counter and pay before being given my food. I was not being singled out for advance payment. Anyone sitting at the tables was required to ante up at serving. I suppose this regulation was to keep the opposite-side diners from drifting out the back door before settling their accounts. With Charlie trapped in his tiny area of operations at the front, he was in no position to go after deadbeats.

Having paid my thirty-five cents (twenty-five for the burger, ten for the beverage, no tip expected), I would carry the burger and drink back to the tiny table and enter a zone that was as close to heaven as food will take an adolescent boy. Charlie's cheeseburger was something else, a large, juicy, cheesy mound of meat encased in an enormous bun with catsup, mustard, and any other condiment you might want readily available. As for my choice to pair with the cheeseburger, the Chocolate Soldier was the obvious winner from Charlie's beverage selections, which also included Coca-Cola, RC Cola, and Orange Crush soda, as well as tea or coffee.

My consumption routine never varied. I'd chew on the properly warm burger, savoring the combination of flavors, then take a drag of the semi-milky, chocolaty brew, then do it all over again until it was gone, much too soon, when I'd regretfully get up, wave goodbye to Charlie and head out for the Scout meeting at The Point Baptist Church, thirty-five cents poorer but infinitely richer in terms of experience and enjoyment.

At the church, I'd leave my bike in the rack next to the assembly building and go inside to find one or two Scoutmasters and anywhere from a dozen to two dozen members of our troop wandering in, some carrying projects they'd brought to get validation for a merit badge. Occasionally, someone would actually show up wearing the full uniform. Most of us, however, wore partials, usually jeans with whatever part of the uniform we bothered to put on. Some of the troop couldn't afford the uniforms, which weren't cheap and could be bought only in the kids' section of one of the better of the downtown department stores. Most just preferred jeans and a regulation shirt to the full kit.

Pretty much on time, the Scoutmaster would call the roll and collect our weekly dues of a quarter, indicating that the meeting was beginning. The next hour to an hour-and-a-half was spent in a generally unstructured way, maybe reading a booklet that specified the requirements for whatever merit badge you were trying to win at the time or showing the Scoutmaster your project or proof of completion from a schoolteacher. (My art teacher, for example, had signed off on my preparedness for the Art badge.) There was always a lot of good-natured horsing around. Just before time to go, the Scoutmaster would announce anything we needed to know before the next meeting.

Then I'd ride my bike the block back to the more-commercial strip of The Point to look over the comic books at the drug store and get a Coke, usually with a couple of my buddies along. None of my friends who regularly came to meetings lived close to me, so once we'd finished with that, we'd split up, riding our bikes in different directions. In summertime, it would be early twilight when we headed home. In winter, however, it was pitch dark. None of the lights on my bikes ever worked exactly the way they were supposed to, but it didn't matter because there were several street lights on each of the five blocks I had to ride to reach the house, and the Donald Duck episode had taught me to be super careful.

Back home, I'd sprawl on my bed and empty the contents of my pockets to see how much of my $2.50 allowance was left. It always surprised me how fast the money went. Thirty-five cents at Charlie's, a quarter for my Scout dues, maybe another twenty cents at the drug store. Whoa – I'd spent eighty cents. That left me only $1.70 for the rest of the week. Sometimes, it would hit me that maybe I needed to cut back on some part of my Friday routine, and for a couple of weeks I might just *look* at the comic books at the drug store. But I never failed to pay my Scout dues, and I never gave up Charlie's and the cheeseburgers and the Chocolate Soldiers.

CHAPTER EIGHTEEN

ONE SUMMER'S WORK UP IN SMOKE

At last, seventh grade was done, and we were out for the summer. The next week I celebrated my thirteenth birthday and got a surprise twenty tucked into a card from an aunt. My first stop in the quest to spend this loot was Shepard's Shoe Shop to replenish my stock of ten-cent balsa-wood gliders. It was then that I realized these lightweight craft, the staple of my childhood play, had lost their allure. The new fad within my small group of model-building geeks was "stick built" airplanes. These wood, paper and metal kits came in a dizzying array of styles. Some were based on World War I or World War II prototypes, others on civilian aviation types.

There were various ways to power these flying models, among them gas-powered engines and the ever-popular rubber band. Some of the models were just gliders, without any power source. My choice for this first stick-built was a powered glider, somewhat of a hybrid. It was a model of an early German experimental jet-propelled "aeroplane" from the 1920s, intended to be powered by a tiny jet engine (which had to be bought separately).

Why this particular model? I liked the look of it on the box cover. Not only was it interesting, but it looked fairly simple in design, giving the illusion that it would be simple to build. So I bought it. For his project, Vernon, my primary partner in model building as

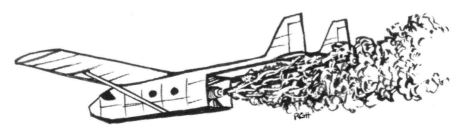

---

in so many other hobbies and endeavors, had chosen a plain old Piper Cub rubber-band powered model. I recall feeling a bit superior.

The two of us began building our planes on Vernon's screened porch. Thanks to his long-suffering mother, we each had a battered card table for a work space and privacy for concentration. I *needed* to concentrate. I had built only plastic-and-solid-wood airplane models before. This was my introduction into the big-time stick-built world. First, there were about a million (not much of an exaggeration) tiny, fragile balsa-wood parts. Many had to be cut out of a printed sheet of thin wood, others were to be cut to fit from a bundle of flimsy strips of wood. The box label touted "No Instructions Needed!" Which meant very little, as it turned out, save that the designer thought whoever bought the kit knew as much as he did. What *was* included was a full-size diagram of the plane printed on thin tissue paper.

I looked hard at this thin-tissue diagram, and began construction in earnest. Cutting, fitting, gluing, and cussing continued for days. At last I had a recognizable model, but my work was by no means done. Once the basic framework was finished, the tissuing and doping process was begun. What that means is that these models were to be covered with tissue paper glued over the wooden skeleton, after which the tissue was sprayed with water. When dry, the tissue became stretched and taut. At that point, the "dope" – a clear, very volatile varnish – had to be painted over the tissue to protect and strengthen it. (I go into this detail as FYI for those who've never built one of these nerve-wracking, complicated and fragile things.)

Finally, after what seemed like way-too-much careful handiwork, given how simple the box cover had made the model look, the plane was complete. Except, of course, for the jet engine. To get this advanced propulsion device, Vernon and I had to take the bus downtown to the only full-service hobby shop. We asked for the engine by number, and when the sales clerk produced it, we were shocked. This little gem was indeed a Jetex solid-fuel propelled unit, but it was *tiny*, much smaller than I expected. Still, I could hardly wait to ride the bus home, install the Jetex on the model, and try it out.

Before proceeding with actual installation, we decided to test the engine, so we clamped it to the picnic table in Vernon's backyard and set to work. You had to open the three-inch-long tube body of the engine and insert a solid cylinder of jet fuel, along with a two-inch fuse. You then put the propulsion cap (that's what it was called) over the open end with the fuse sticking out of a tiny hole in the cap. Then we lit the fuse, jumped back and watched as the little aluminum cylinder spewed out copious amounts of white smoke. Hot damn – it looked *good*. The only question now was, would it push my plane into flight? Vernon was doubtful, saying that he was glad his Piper Cub depended on good, old rubber-band power.

Once the jet engine was cool enough to handle, we reloaded it with fuel and fuse. Then we mounted it into the body of my beautiful creation, which called for the engine to be screwed to a wood block that was glued to the floor of the plane.

We were ready. Our legs pumped furiously as – steering with one hand and holding our planes with the other – we biked the three blocks to the football field at the high school, a venue we used frequently for testing one thing and another. Parking the bikes, we walked onto the field, each gingerly holding our soon-to-be-airborne beauties. The day was warm and still, good launching weather. Both of us were keen to see this new marvel of miniature technology in action, and we'd already agreed that I was to take off first.

The time had come, and it was a significant time. To bring this breathtakingly perfect model into existence, I'd put up with a lot of tedium on pretty summer days when other, more-immediately-enjoyable pursuits had beckoned. Once or twice along the way, I'd had my doubts, but now that I was here, standing in the end zone, facing the full length of the field, about to taste the fruits of genuine accomplishment, I knew that it had been worth every minute. As I held my plane at shoulder height, Vernon reached around me and, with his father's trusty Zippo, lit the fuse. I waited until I could hear the whoosh of the smoke from the rear of the plane, then launched it into the air.

It was up! I felt like cheering. Away it flew, about ten feet off the ground, straight towards the fifty-yard line. What a sight! The sunlight glinted off its shiny wings, the smoke trail was haloed by the afternoon light. It was a classic moment. Then it was over. At about the seventy-five-yard line, she blew! No explosion – just a slight puff of smoke and flame – but she was gone. We raced up the field to the smoldering grass spot that was all that remained of my summer's work. It turned out that airplanes made of varnished tissue paper and glue-laden balsa-wood burn extremely well, and fast. Once we stomped out the growing grass fire, all we found was the guilty device, the little Jetex engine, blackened but ready to go again. Vernon looked at the mess thoughtfully and decided to launch his creation another day.

Lacking the mental energy to ride, we trudged back to Vernon's place, pushing our bikes for the slow, silent return. It had been a sobering day; and we had a lot to think about.

I guess the main moral I got out of this sad tale is that you had better enjoy the "doing" of a project as much as you anticipate the ultimate rewards. Because the rewards may be long in coming and short in duration.

CHAPTER NINETEEN

THE HMS "OLD LEAKY"

Vernon and I were pretty depressed at the abrupt end to my great stick-built experiment the summer we were thirteen. Even the annual visit to my grandparents hadn't cheered me up, so it was a treat when on my return Mr. Campbell, Vernon's father, took us fishing on a stream that was all that remained of a large lake. He told us that the lake had been part of a real-estate development that had collapsed, leading to the lake being drained years before. Now, the old lake bed was little more than an overgrown jungle-like forest with the stream meandering through it.

We had a terrific time; and, after this visit to "drown some worms," as Mr. Campbell put it, we were determined to return and navigate the whole extent of the former lake's watercourse. We calculated that, if you measured the lake by driving the length of it, it might have been about two or three miles long. We could have borrowed Mr. Campbell's boat or even rented one, but Vernon and I decided to make the excursion more interesting by building our own.

Such an undertaking was not unique for us. Over the years, we had worked together to build many projects, mostly models and other small items. The largest vehicle-type project had been a push car made of wood, tin, old buggy wheels, broomsticks and an abandoned GMC steering wheel that we'd found in one of our periodic alley scavengings. This little gem had brakes of a crude sort,

rope-guided steering and – thanks to my mother – a padded seat. We launched this one-of-a-kind car down the hill at the end of my street about a hundred times, which worked well save for the necessity to push it back up to the starting point each of those times.

So, as we started our boat-building project, Vernon and I were hardly novices in the custom-construction game. It helped that Mr. Campbell had a workshop built as a shed addition to his garage that was well equipped with woodworking tools. The craft was to be about seven feet in length and about three feet wide, a respectable but not unwieldy size on the face of it. We envisioned it as somewhat squared off, but with a sloped bow.

Finding the wood was the first requirement. I furnished a few odds and ends of ¼" plywood and 2 x 4s, while Vernon talked his neighbor out of an almost full 4x8 sheet of plywood. We conveniently ignored the fact that none of the plywood was waterproof.

The construction took about a week of after-school work sessions. The more we worked, the more complicated the process became. Mr. Campbell came by to check on our progress, but quickly walked away, shaking his head. We were a little offended. I'll admit the emerging craft wasn't a thing of beauty, but it was ours and we persevered. We were generous in our attempts to get it stream-worthy, using at least a gallon of gooey, sticky, black roofing cement to caulk up all our badly made seams. Then, at last, we were ready to paint our craft a bilious green, and she was – we felt – ready to float.

After consultation with Mr. Campbell, who was to take us to the put-in point and retrieve us a couple of hours later at the old dam at the south end of the lake bed, we selected a Saturday for the big launch day. We had to push the boat halfway into the trunk and hope the rope we tied it on with would hold during the tense, five-mile trip to the lake, our fragile craft bouncing behind as we watched nervously through the rear window.

At the launch site, we eased the boat into the murky water for its maiden voyage. At least it floated. We then loaded our supplies: two homemade paddles, one BB gun, a hunting knife, and lunch, which consisted of peanut-butter and grape-jelly sandwiches, apples, Baby Ruth candy bars, and four canned orange sodas. This was our favorite lunch at that time in our lives, consisting as it did of all the major kid food groups.

We waved back to Mr. Campbell, who was somewhat speculatively watching us begin to move, and pushed off into the unknown. We were away! This was going to be great!

The creek followed a twisty course through the heavily overgrown woods that had sprung up in the rich soil of the drained lake bed. Things went exactly as expected at first. After about half an hour, however, we began to notice that water was oozing through our carefully caulked seams in several places.

Vernon snorted, "Where's the bailing can?"

"What bailing can?" I asked.

All of a sudden, we both glared, each silently blaming the other for this oversight. The current was moving us slowly through the curvy channel. The situation was irritating, but not exactly dangerous, for the stream was never more than about twenty feet wide at any point.

The leaking picked up momentum, so we began paddling to increase our speed. I guess we thought we could outrun our leaks. Unfortunately, the faster we paddled, the more muddy water we splashed into the boat.

Finally, the decision was made to pull on shore at a low sand bar and empty water out by tipping the boat over. The only problem with this strategy was that the sand bar turned out to be a mud bar, and as soon as we jumped out, we sank up to our knees in black, oozy, slimy mud. Well, mud-sunk or not, we were already committed to a course of action, so we tugged the boat up onto the semi-solid mud and began to tip it over. Just then we realized that our supplies were still in the boat. I grabbed the BB gun while Vernon went for the knife and one paddle. Everything else fell into either the water or the mud. We scrambled over the boat to try and save the lunch box, but to no avail. Because of the weight of the orange sodas (already eagerly anticipated due to our thirst from all that paddling), the metal box quickly sank out of sight. The other paddle escaped the situation and drifted quietly away, but we weren't too concerned because we thought we might catch up with it later.

"Maybe we should feel around for the lunch box," I hesitantly suggested.

"You can if you want to, but I'm not eating or drinking anything that's been in that water," Vernon retorted.

Covered in mud, thirsty, our mood rapidly deteriorating even further, we reboarded "Old Leaky," as we'd now rechristened the boat, and our journey continued. Almost immediately we began to miss the lost lunch box, which, along with its energy-giving contents and our only drinkable liquid, was almost certainly resting on the bottom of the murky stream. We also regretted the loss of the second paddle, which must have floated far ahead for we never saw it again.

We'd already realized that, with all the stream's twists, turns and double backs, the trip was easily twice what we'd thought it would be, and by now our spirits were really ebbing low. The encroaching undergrowth began to arch over the creek, creating a low green tunnel through which we had to paddle. All of a sudden, on a low branch just ahead, a rather large snake slid off into the water and swam away.

We took this as a sign that we needed to be more vigilant regarding what might lie around us in the swamp, so I hefted the trusty BB gun at an upward angle in the bow while Vernon rowed and steered with the remaining paddle. The remainder of the trip, however, was relatively incident free. We did have to tip the boat again, but after our earlier experience, we made sure we were on firmer ground and there was no loss of equipment.

After what seemed like days, we began to hear traffic sounds from up ahead. Hopefully, we were approaching the road that crossed the old dam because we weren't sure of how much more of this we could take. In about ten or fifteen minutes, we saw through the undergrowth the glint of sun off of a car. Rounding the last bend of the green-tunneled stream, our soggy little craft emerged into bright sunlight, where we saw Mr. Campbell dozing in the Chevy fastback. He awoke as we were pulling Old Leaky out of the water.

"Well, I see you boys had an interesting trip. You know,

you've been gone about four hours."

This innocent comment was met with silence from both of us. We were itching, hungry and, most of all, thirsty. As we tied the boat to the car, Vernon announced that that was the last boat he would ever step into, *ever*. I wasn't sure about that broad a generalization, but I silently agreed that I would never step into *that* boat again.

After he had heard our tale of adventure and disaster, not to mention impending starvation and dehydration, Mr. Campbell drove us to his favorite barbeque drive-in. As we filled up on sandwiches and iced colas, we made the formal decision to decommission our plywood nightmare. It moldered behind the Campbell garage for a while, and then one day we realized it had disappeared.

CHAPTER TWENTY

FAIR GAMES

One of the few things that compensated for our having to go back to school in the fall was that the State Fair arrived just a few weeks later. Luckily, my house was only a long walk to the State Fairgrounds. All kids looked forward to the fair, each for his or her own reasons – the midway rides, the junk-food concessions, the freak shows, the model-train exhibits, and even the agricultural exhibits. For me and Vernon, however, the primary lure of the fair was *gambling*. There was no sort of gambling available to the kids in my neighborhood. About the best you could do was to bet each other that you would get a better grade on the math test on Friday. The bet might be money, food, or some prized possession. The real problem was collecting if you won.

Fair Week offered a much wider scope to boys with enterprise and a plan. Every fall, Vernon and I would be taken separately to the fair by our parents, usually early in the week. Afterwards, we would get together and compare notes on the games of chance we had seen. We then began to prepare our return trip, which we were allowed to make without adult supervision as long as we followed certain rules. The year we were thirteen we progressed from simply *discussing* which games might be easier to win to an actual *practicing* of the midway games of chance in order to hone our techniques. We found that setting up home versions of the games was a real challenge, and setting up some of them was beyond us for one reason

or another – the shooting-gallery-type games, for example. Our Red Ryder BB guns were nothing like the rifles used in the various shooting galleries, and we couldn't figure out what to do about the kind of targets the midway games employed. We felt, however, that we could actually master pitching pennies into plates, throwing balls at milk bottles, and tossing rings over wood stakes (at least as long as our mothers didn't go looking for their embroidery hoops or certain of their everyday dishes). In our opinion, practice, practice, *practice* was the key, and we approached this with a zeal that seemed both to amuse and irritate our parents.

Once we felt we were ready to take on the carnies, we set off the next afternoon for the fair, prepared – as we saw it at the time – to avenge all the poor rubes who'd been taken in by these slicksters. We always walked the approximately three-quarters of a mile because there was no safe place to stow our bikes at the Fairgrounds. In our pockets, we usually had about five or six dollars apiece that had to serve for both our gambling stake and any other expenses we might incur. Once we'd paid our fifty-cents admission, before we could get down to the business at hand, we had to check in at the Central Methodist Church food booth, where my Aunt Olene was a volunteer, and get a hot dog or a piece of cake. My mother said it was a safe place for us to eat and not get food poisoning. Unfortunately, what I really wanted were corn dogs – as many as I could stuff down, while Vernon leaned more toward colorful snow cones.

Our first quest of the afternoon was the huge Lionel train layout in the Industrial Arts Building. Since we were both train enthusiasts, we never missed this spectacle. It was sponsored by Mack's, owned by my parents' old friends. Mack's was the city's largest sporting goods store, the one with the super hobby department. I think the layout was the same year after year; but, since it only came into being once a year, that didn't matter much. It was an awe-inspiring sight for those of us whose layouts were limited by normal room dimensions.

Next we headed to the midway to check out the rides and sideshows. Since I tend to get queasy when violent movement is involved, I have never gone in for carnival rides, probably a particularly wise policy at the fair since I was always full of corn dogs and orangeade. Vernon, however, liked to ride and usually paid out precious cash for a turn on the Dive Bomber, a two-cabin, twirling, vertical, end-over-end contraption that I could barely stand to watch.

The sideshows were always interesting *looking*, although we only went to one that I remember. The barker really had us going with his spiel, and we anted up fifty cents each for a look at some crummily staged torture and murder scenes from history. The fifty cents had *not* been well spent, we agreed afterwards – what a letdown! On the other hand, we always enjoyed watching the girly-show come-on, largely because this was the closest we would get to the actual show, given our age. The ladies were paraded out in front of the entrance for the crowd's approval, wearing short sequined costumes. Boom-bada-boom music would blare over the urging of the barker, and the ladies would shake their sequins. Once the barker had the guys pumped up enough to reach for their wallets, he would send the ladies inside to "get into something more comfortable," an expression we found of interest. Then the tickets to this promised paradise were sold for the next performance, starting in ten minutes. We never made it to an actual show. By the time we were old enough for legal admission, we'd moved on to dating girls who, even without the sequins, were more our speed.

It was as the ladies returned inside that we realized that we'd better get on with our true purpose in coming. Our fair time was limited, as we had to be home before dark, so we knew that the hour had come for us to put our game strategy to a real-world test.

The first game we tried was the hoop toss. The prize we wanted was, believe it or not, a live goldfish in a plastic bag of water. For some reason that wasn't totally clear to us even at the time, we thought this was a wonderful prize, and we determined to give the game our all. Our hoop-tossing method was to pitch the hoop upwards, not horizontally. The cost was twenty-five cents for three hoops. Vernon went first. He hit the goldfish stake on the second hoop but missed the third. I'll admit I was nervous as I stepped up to pay my quarter, possibly because Vernon's win had intensified the competition between us. As Vernon clutched his fish, grinning his lopsided grin, I tossed my first hoop at the same prize – missed. Second hoop – missed again. Vernon began to snicker and roll his eyes. Third hoop went up and away. No good! I was determined to get a fish. Another quarter on the counter and a sly, knowing look from the carnie. He knew he had a sucker. The fourth hoop flew up but too far to the right. Plop, the hoop landed on the stake for a cigarette lighter.

Well, it wasn't a goldfish, but a kid can always use a lighter, if only to set off fireworks. Vernon wasn't so snide now. I had accidentally won a pretty good prize. My last two hoops bounced off into the back of the tent, so I gave it up, pocketed my lighter (it never worked) and moved on to new gambling ventures.

Our next skill challenge, we decided, would be the penny-toss game. We were surprised that the game was ten cents a toss. I don't know why we thought it was a penny. Well, we had the money and were committed, as well as practiced, so we decided to go for it. After all, we'd worked out our system with pennies, not that different in weight and size from dimes, so we should be OK.

Vernon, a math whiz, could calculate trajectories like mad, and our practical research based on his theories had shown us that a low-level, horizontal pitch was all wrong. The coin would hit a plate and skip right off. After trying various approaches, what we settled on was an underhanded upward toss, so the coin came down on the plate from above. Even if the coin bounced off the rimless plate, it had a chance of landing on another, maybe not the one you wanted, but a prize is a prize.

After we each changed a half dollar into dimes, we studied

the game layout, relating it to what we'd practiced. The plates stood in offset rows, mounted on metal poles. On each pole under the plate was a number, one through ten. These numbers corresponded to the shelves that exhibited the prizes available for each number. There were some crummy prizes, as you might guess. Stupid plastic canes with a feather stuck on the end, ratty little teddy bears in strange fluorescent colors, girly hair clips and, worst of all, a green-and-pink plastic parrot on a perch. I had my eye on row eight, especially the jaunty plaster sailor. He reminded me of the Cracker Jack logo. Cracker Jack being one of my favorite snacks, I decided I had to have this piece of advertising art.

My first throw was too low; the dime went under the number-eight plate and almost hit the number-four, the hair clip – a close call. Second throw was again wild; it went nowhere. I had to calm down and remember the practice games. Third throw was up high as it should be; it hit the number-eight plate but bounced off into the back curtain. I was now down thirty cents with no results. Vernon stepped up, handed me his fish and made his first throw. Again, the house won. He also threw too low. His second throw hit the number-nine plate and stayed. He was the unproud owner of a mint-green, eight-inch teddy bear, which was almost as bad as the hair clip or the plastic parrot. He pleaded with the much-amused carnie to let him trade for something else, to no avail. The carnie handed over the bear, which Vernon immediately stuffed inside his shirt in case someone he knew might see him with it. Once the bear was concealed, I handed him his fish and got ready to try again. Sure, his prize had been crummy, but at least he'd won something.

By now I was up to my fourth throw, aiming yet again at number-eight. Close but no good. Forty cents down. This was getting expensive. OK, this was it, one more dime, I decided, and I was done. Fifth throw – a high arching trajectory, hitting the number-one plate (the awful plastic cane prize) but bouncing over to, and landing on, number eight, where it stayed. FINALLY, the prize I yearned for, the sailor, was mine. Grabbing it from the fifty-cent-richer carnie, I realized it was bigger and heavier than I had imagined. As we walked away, Vernon with his fish and the green bear stuffed in his shirt and me with my increasingly heavy sailor shifted from one hand to the other, I began to wonder if my fifty cents had been well spent. I couldn't help wondering, too, how many boxes of Cracker Jack I could have bought for fifty cents, each with a prize of its own. Over the years, there had been one or two decent prizes from good old Jack. Still, no point crying over dimes lost. We had to get on with our plan.

Our next much-practiced game was throwing baseballs at stacked milk bottles. However, we quickly realized that the so-called milk bottles at the actual game stand were made of some sort of heavy ceramic material, not the lightweight, fragile, glass sort that we'd used for toss practice at home. Even so, we were game. After all, a principle was a principle. We'd just have to throw *harder*. I set my sailor down between my feet, paid my twenty-five cents for three balls, and looked over the available prizes. A particularly lustrous pink-tinted pitcher caught my eye. It would be a present for my mother, I decided. I wound up for my first throw. High and away – not a single bottle touched. Second pitch – *missed again*! Well, this was it – the last ball. I really wound up and let fly. The ball hit a stack of three bottles but just bounced off. I looked disbelievingly at the booth attendant. He just shrugged and said, "Ya better throw harder next time." There would not, however, be a next time. I retrieved my sailor, asked Vernon if he was going to try some balls, and started to move on. He considered the setup and my last throw and in his understated way said, "Nah, they ain't got anything worth trying for."

Leaving this unsatisfying booth and its disappointed huckster, we passed a couple of games that we considered beneath our skill levels, especially the one requiring only that the player retrieve a floating yellow duckling from a small watercourse so that the operator could look at the number stenciled on its bottom and hand over the prize related to that number. That, we decided immediately, was for pre-schoolers. As for the darts-and-balloon tent, that was in our view strictly for girls. Wandering along, sucking on lukewarm sodas, we decided to make another circuit of the main midway before starting for home. Both of us had a little money left, for corn dogs if nothing else. Vernon was still lugging his goldfish, and his shirt bulged with the crummy little teddy bear. I asked him what he was going to do with his teddy. He considered the question for a second and said, "Target practice." I knew the little teddy was in for a rough life, probably of brief duration. Heading back toward the midway, we passed the merry-go-round and the Ferris wheel – both of which we considered kiddie rides. We thought about going into the Crazy Mirror maze, but the canvas signs for the Alligator Man, the one-thousand-pound woman, the rubber man and the monkey boy drew our attention. (Like most boys, we were sorely deficient in political correctness.) After due consideration, however, we passed, figuring they were probably all fake like the murder/torture exhibit we had been suckered into earlier.

A roaring din to our left drew us in that direction. The "World's Largest Motor Thrill Arena" came into sight around the side of the tilt–a-whirl ride. *This* was something we both were interested in – motorcycles. With some difficulty, the barker was trying to be heard over the screaming roar of three big motorcycles on a platform in front of a towering wood-and-steel circular arena. Two men and a woman were astride these massive machines, whose rear wheels were on static rollers so they could rev up the engines to screaming RPMs. After a few ear-splitting minutes they eased off the throttles and rolled the bikes from the platform into the arena. The next show was about to begin. We were hooked. This had better be good – it cost us seventy-five cents each for a ticket.

We then toiled up the flimsy stairs that led to the viewing area above the wooden arena bowl. We took our places, excitedly looking down into the arena. This would be an *excellent* spot from which to observe the action.

The show was not a letdown. We saw bone-rattling exhibitions of man (and woman) against gravity. The daredevils inside the circular arena drove their bikes faster and faster and began to climb up the almost-vertical, vibrating wooden walls toward where the stunned audience gaped down at them. The kicker was when a woman stunt rider rose from her seat behind one of the drivers, climbed up on his shoulders and stood up – all while going in a tight circle at a ninety-degree angle from the ground. A very satisfactory seventy-five-cent expenditure, we agreed.

With our bones still vibrating, we wobbled towards the rear gate of the fairgrounds. It was getting darker, and we had to head home. Vernon's fish was not looking good. It needed more fresh water, and soon. About 300 yards from the fairgrounds was a large creek (which the city was trying to turn into a drainage canal) that we sometimes played in and around. Vernon considered what to do about the fish – we didn't think it would last until we got home. After a moment of deliberation, the fish was liberated from its plastic cell into the creek's dubious waters.

Fishless, we wandered the last few blocks homeward, I with my seemingly ten-pound sailor and my shiny cigarette lighter, Vernon with his still-hidden green teddy bear. After this, fair-wise, the only thing we had to look forward to was the fireworks display at ten P.M. every night. We each could see most of the higher color bursts from our respective houses.

This was the only year we tried to outsmart the carnival professionals. In subsequent years, we just looked, wished and ate our way through the brightly lit, sawdust-paved midway.

CHAPTER TWENTY-ONE

THE GLADIATOR'S REVENGE

Maybe it was the fiasco of Old Leaky, but Vernon and I left the experimental-project building alone for a while. This wasn't as much of a sacrifice as it might have been earlier, as school was about to go back in session. Still, all work and no play wasn't a possibility for me, so about a month and a half into the school year, when some of the neighbor kids came by one Saturday to see if I wanted to play Romans vs. Gladiators, I was in and grabbed one of our metal garbage-can lids before taking off.

It was Mrs. Miller's history class that gave us the idea of reenacting this long-ago and distant rivalry, but the venue was strictly local: the creek bank at the three-block-distant foot of the street that ran in front of my house. Once there, we chose as the battle site a drainage ditch leading across undeveloped land to the creek. There were a couple of reasons for this. For one thing, at this time of year there was an abundance of dried goldenrod plants all around, and

their stems, pulled from the ever-present mud, could serve as our spears. For another, the ditch provided a natural demarcation point for the opposing forces, with the Roman Centurions on one side of the ditch and the Gladiators on the other, three kids to a side. The costuming consisted of metal garbage-can lids that everyone had brought from home, a couple of ill-fitting football hel-

mets and a baseball cap. Some of us – including me, of course – were without head protection. I'd only recently started wearing glasses, and it bugged me to have anything else on my head.

The attack mode was to take a pulled-up, dried goldenrod stem and its muddy roots and throw it in the manner of a spear directly at the opponent, who would raise his shield to try to keep it from hitting him. It was all good fun for a while, the clang and splat of the "spears" against the metal shields proving highly satisfactory. It was half an hour into this ancient warfare before we had our first casualty. Unfortunately, it was me. I guess my left-arm coordination was off due to my Donald Duck bike accident a few years earlier, just up the road, but I didn't raise my shield quite high enough when an especially big incoming goldenrod spear was headed toward me – or maybe my glasses slipped and I misjudged the trajectory. Either way, the mud-tipped missile slid just over my shield and hit me square in the right ear.

Mud and blood are not a good mix, especially in the ear. The battle stopped, and a truce was instituted. Not to assess the damage to my ear, but to come up with a plausible reason for coming home with a garbage-can lid and a muddy, bloody ear. The selected story was to tell my parents that I had a fall from my bike and landed on my right side in a muddy bank. To make this look better, the guys took turns applying mud to my right leg and arm. I then had to bike home uphill, while one of the Romans headed up the alley with the garbage-can lid, which he was to replace on the can at the back of our garage.

It worked. I'd have felt more comfortable with the whole scenario if I'd had longer to rehearse it, but when I got home I found that my mother had already come in from her job as a drugstore manager. I had no choice; I had to wing it. After her initial shock over my pitiful condition, she cleaned my ear to see if it needed further medical attention. To my great relief, she decided that the cleaning and painful antiseptic washing she'd administered had done the trick – I wouldn't have to go to the hospital! Since my mother was naturally inclined to rush me to the hospital on any pretext, this was a victory for my own determination never to set foot in one again.

I felt very pleased with myself and not at all guilty or contrite. Sure, the guys and I shouldn't have been throwing stuff at one another, but at least we had the smarts to concoct a plausible cover story when we screwed up - and what our parents didn't know wouldn't hurt them. I'd lived to fight another day and all without benefit of one of those dreaded trips to the Emergency Room. Anyway, it had been a while since I'd gotten hurt doing something like that. The guys up the street and I weren't playing the games based on history lessons or movies nearly as often as we had even a few months before. As for Vernon, he'd always been more into experimenting in the real world, and there was plenty there to keep us occupied.

CHAPTER TWENTY-TWO

THE HOMEMADE ZEPPELIN

Eighth grade was proceeding the same way as earlier grades. I drew book-report covers, memorized the names and locations of foreign capitals, and slid down in my seat whenever the teacher wanted anyone to come to the board to diagram a sentence or work a math equation. I got A's in Art and Reading and B's most of the time in everything else, with an occasional A mixed in for Science. I wasn't the best student, and I wasn't the worst, and school for the most part held little interest. Vernon, who was half a grade ahead of me, was more busy with schoolwork than usual that fall, and it was springtime before we got back to the business that had preoccupied us for much of our boyhood to that point: the production of dozens of model aircraft of various types and complexities, from solid-wood display models to large, stick-built, tow-line gliders.

The Zeppelin idea grew out of a trip to Ivey's, the West End five-and-dime that had traditionally supplied our lust for new aircraft adventures. There, among the Comet, Monogram, and Strombecker offerings, was a plastic model of the German Zeppelin *Hindenburg*, of the famous 1930s disaster at Lakewood, New Jersey. We discussed purchasing the kit, but it seemed odd to have a static, sit-on-a-table airship. It was Vernon who came up with the idea of designing and building an actual operating Zeppelin of our own.

Mr. Ivey, the store owner and presider over the balcony hobby counter, was not pleased at our decision not to buy anything that day, since he had come up to the balcony to entice us into purchasing something from his reduced-for-quick-sale stock. Mr. Ivey's sale stock, however, no longer tempted us, consisting as it did of boxes and boxes of sooty, singed, and smoke-damaged car, airplane and boat models – the result of a localized fire in the rear of the store some months earlier. He would really push the kids to buy these models. The price was usually half off what was marked on the old, peeling tags. The only drawback to these bargains was that the boxes were taped shut and you bought them as is, no inspection allowed. After one or two such purchases, you found that the plastic parts had deformed into abstract shapes, visually interesting but unsuited to a satisfactory model-building experience.

Once the idea of a Zeppelin of our own began to ferment in our minds, the materials needed to be located, or adapted. The first consideration was the envelope or bag or body of the ship. As we mulled this over, I suddenly had *the idea*. My father worked for a large commercial laundry and dry-cleaning company. Dry cleaning came back in clear plastic bags. I knew from visits to the plant that these bags were cut from a continuous roll of plastic. I would get my father to bring home a long piece of this plastic. I told him that we were going to do an experiment. We were always making something out of junk and found objects, so he rarely questioned our motives and the next day came back with the plastic.

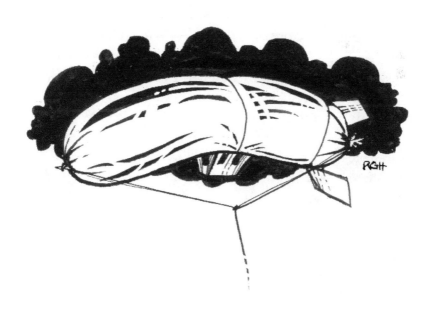

Now we had the material for the gas-bag portion of the ship. Next, we could decide how big to make our Zeppelin. Rolling out the plastic on the lawn at Vernon's house, we decided that the natural diameter of the plastic sleeve – thirty-six inches – would be the diameter of the Zeppelin – and that we'd make it about twelve feet long. We then tied one end of the bag with string and sealed it with glue.

The next day, while his mother was out shopping, Vernon and I took the flat twelve-feet-by-thirty-six-inches plastic bag into his living room, shut off the valve to the gas fireplace logs, disconnected the hose, stuck it into the bag, and turned the gas back on. It seemed to take forever to fill, and we impatiently watched the irregular inflation of what looked increasingly like a twelve-by-three-foot plastic sausage. Finally, the bag looked full; and we reconnected the gas hose to the logs, sealed the bag, and checked to make sure it was working all right.

Our next challenge was getting the softly inflated bag out of the gas-infused living room and through the front door; and we managed it only by cautious maneuvering and some innovative twisting and turning. As we did this, it seemed to me that the smell of gas was growing stronger. Outside, we each took an end and carried the long plastic sausage down the driveway to the garage and slipped it inside, where it began to drift upwards. When the bag was resting up against the garage rafters, we ran back into the house, opened windows, turned on a portable fan and cleared out the lingering odor of gas. Our makeshift ventilation was successful enough that, when Vernon's mother returned from the A&P, I don't think she suspected anything. (Although by now, you think she'd never have left us in the house at all, given some of the things we did in it over the years.)

The next decision was how to harness this aeronautical wonder. We attached fishing line to the nose and tail and devised a paper-and-cardboard cabin to hang beneath the center of the bag. We wanted to hang fins on the rear, to mimic the pictures we'd seen, but this kept giving us problems. Nothing could be glued to the thin plastic itself, so – unable to devise an alternative – we regretfully gave up on the fins.

The next day we decided to give the Zeppelin its trial flight. There were too many trees around Vernon's house, so, suspending the Zeppelin between us, we hauled it the three blocks to the high-school football field, usual site of any of our experiments too massive to be accommodated at either of our houses. We could see a couple of neighbors peeking out their windows as we passed, but I guess Vernon's reputation for experimentation – and his temper when his projects were interfered with – kept them indoors.

Once on the field, we let out the attached line, and the ship rose majestically into the warm late-springtime air. We let out about 200 more feet of fishing line and watched as the almost-clear bag of gas just hung there with its little cabin swinging underneath. The thing stayed up, but it was not a satisfactory trial. It didn't look like a Zeppelin, just a plastic bag shaped like a sausage on a string. It was actually pretty pathetic, and we soon decided to haul it down and scrap the project.

We parked the Zeppelin in Vernon's garage for the night, and began to debate its fate. Nothing was settled immediately. Even though we knew we weren't satisfied with it, we still thought that maybe we could salvage it in some way. The next day our hand was forced when we noticed that the clear plastic sausage had begun to sag – it was losing gas. The little cabin had fallen off because of the sagging. Vernon announced that our Zeppelin should be put out of its misery, and I had to agree. His plan was to send it on a free-flying death journey, which sounded pretty interesting.

The how of the death flight was easy. We put a TNT firecracker under the center of the ship, where the cabin had been attached. The only problem remaining was the need for a long fuse to ignite the TNT, and Vernon, as usual, devised a solution. He soaked a long piece of hemp string in diluted roofing cement. When it dried, we attached it to the firecracker fuse and sat back to wait for daylight to fade. At last, twilight came, and we trudged back to the football field for the final Zeppelin flight. Luckily, we remembered to bring along a book of matches. Vernon lit the long fuse as I held the ship in check. The fuse lit, I let go, and she eased up toward a clear, moonless springtime sky. Soon we couldn't see the ship anymore. Even the fuse spark was invisible. We waited and waited, scanning the sky, wondering if the fuse had failed. After what seemed a half-hour – I guess it was actually just minutes – she blew.

It was a very satisfactory result. Just as we'd hoped, the Zeppelin had moved off to our left, over a residential area where several of our friends lived, an area so aware of the Red Menace that had been hanging over everybody since the Russians set off their first atom bomb in 1949 that it was known to harbor at least three or four backyard bomb shelters. The explosion's effect was highly gratifying, a flash and boom followed by a mushrooming blue-gas fireball that quickly dissipated. Our expectation was that nervous householders would see the Zeppelin explosion and report it as an invading Russian aircraft or maybe even a UFO. We were big into UFOs. We scanned the newspaper the next day, but found nothing. If anyone saw the explosion, they didn't report it. Ah well, fame is fleeting, as was our Zeppelin.

CHAPTER TWENTY-THREE
INVENTION OF THE FIRST DIRT BIKE

Considering that I was an only child and was, further-more, according to everyone who voiced an opinion on the subject, spoiled rotten, it seems odd to me now that I never got one of my most wished-for items, a motorbike. Maybe it was because my parents had already had to re-mortgage their home several years before because of the unfortunate incident involving my Official Donald Duck Bicycle. I guess they figured if I could do that much damage to myself on a bike, what I was likely to do on a motorbike was something they preferred to avoid. In any event, I don't remember pushing them too hard on the issue, maybe because I knew it was a lost cause.

My buddy Vernon also yearned for some sort of motorized transportation in these pre-car years, but for once his parents also dug in their heels and failed to produce what he wanted. Our response was to try to make our good old pedal bikes look and sound like real motorbikes. First, we addressed the sound issue. We were trying for a rich vroom-vroom. Our approach was to clip some plastic cards to the bike frame so that they engaged the wheel spokes. The cards, not surprisingly, had the drawback of a short working life, and we had to replace them frequently. The effect, however, wasn't too bad, giving a nice roaring sound as we coasted down the hill at the end of my street.

Sound was only half of what we were after, of course, and I – the artist – came up with a brilliant idea. I would paint an engine on cardboard and mount it to the bike frame. Once I'd done this on both our bikes, we thought they looked good, at least from a distance, and it was but the work of an instant to replace the plastic cards on the wheels to regain audio.

Now we had sound and an engine visual, but something was still missing. Suddenly, it hit us. We needed an exhaust trail, a sudden puff of smoke when we were accelerating. Our creative powers were really strained with this problem. One of us, I don't remember who, got the bright idea of hooking up some surplus garden hose to a metal funnel. This funnel would be tied to the frame just behind the handle bars. The hose would loop down past the pedals and end up near the rear sprocket, like an exhaust pipe (refer to diagram #1). To get the

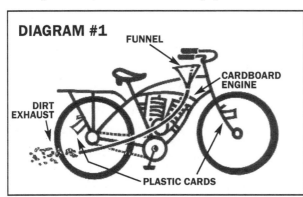

smoke effect, we loaded the funnel with dirt and wood ashes (hence the "first dirt bike"). When we wanted a smoke effect, all we had to do was beat on the funnel to dislodge the dirt and ashes down into the hose and out the rear. I know all this sounds crazy now, but then it seemed to satisfy our needs.

Even so, this fake motorbike phase didn't last long, for we soon began to hatch a plan to circumvent the parental ban on motorized transport.

Vernon had two bikes, one his new Raleigh English type – thin tires, hand brakes and multiple gears – and an old Schwinn that we had used for his fake motorbike makeover. His idea was to convert the older one to a gas engine. With this in mind we biked over to Tubby Watson's father's fix-it shop to talk about motors. The plan called for a small engine with a horizontal drive shaft. This horizontal shaft was needed because the drive was to be a direct friction drive on the rear wheel. Mr. Watson had just the thing – an old motor from a garden tiller.

This weird configuration is hard to explain, so I'll draw it to save a lot of confusing explanations. (See diagram #2)

Weird or not, however, this cobbled-together "motorbike" did work. It got up to about twenty miles per hour on the level, but we had to stay away from hills. The most-dangerous part of a ride was when you needed to stop or slow down fast. You had to remember to raise the "clutch" to disengage the direct drive from the rear wheel.

The cost was economical too. Mr. Watson sold us the engine for five dollars, which we thought was a bargain. As for the other parts, they were all "found" in various garages and junk piles.

This homemade wonder was quite a hit with other kids in the immediate neighborhood, but not with their parents. They particularly objected to its loudness, which made it even better in our estimation. As for mine and Vernon's parents, mine never knew I rode

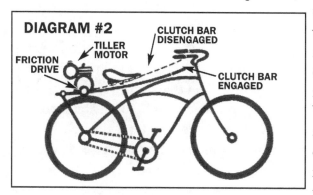

on this motorized wonder because I made a point to stay off my street while roaming around; and Vernon's were so accustomed to his determination to finish his experiments that they just sighed, muttered a subdued "Be careful, son," and looked the other way.

All in all, this one-off invention proved a satisfactory project that summer we were fourteen. It was a transition of sorts and certainly as close as we ever got to a motorcycle.

CHAPTER TWENTY-FOUR

NEVER TRUST YOUR UNCLE

Summers always meant a two-week visit to my grandparents' house in an adjoining state with my cousin Patrick, and the summer I turned fourteen was no different. The only thing that had changed over the years was the mode of transport we used to get to our two weeks of freedom.

Until I was eight, Patrick and I were delivered, after several tedious hours in the back seat of the family Buick, in person by my parents. After that, however, more often than not, we were put on a westward-bound Trailways bus, consigned to the driver, and told to "behave yourselves and stay on the bus until you get there."

Until the summer of my fourteenth year, those visits were kid's play, a time of being allowed to wander on our own through the small, sleepy college town, where everybody knew everybody – and a lot of them seemed to owe our grandfather money or rent their houses from him. Our grandfather understood kid needs. When we first arrived each year, he'd hand each of us a twenty-dollar bill and say offhandedly, "You boys let me know when this is gone." And, when it was, he'd give us another one. This was an arrangement that Patrick and I had always found logistically effective, and as far as we were concerned this relationship with "Andrew Jackson" could have continued indefinitely.

This was the summer, however, when everything changed, for when we arrived, it was announced that we were considered old enough – at fourteen and twelve-and-a-half respectively –

to help Uncle Dick, a general contractor, build houses. Not only were we to work, we were told, but we would actually get PAID!

The idea of really working was foreign to us – Patrick had never had a job and all I'd ever done was to throw papers, but we were game to give it a try, especially since the pay rate was to be fifty cents an hour each. Wow! We figured we might even make twenty dollars a week. Add that to the twenty we usually got, and the total made us giddy.

The real world quickly set in. For one thing, our grandfather didn't hand over the usual twenty. For another, the next day, a Monday, after a hearty breakfast prepared by our Great-Aunt Mae, we were told that Uncle Dick was expecting us on the job site – a small subdivision that he and our grandfather were developing on the back acreage of the eighty-five-year-old family home. At this time, there were about six finished houses and four in various stages of construction.

Dick, my mother's youngest brother, was a kid-friendly type of uncle. He was a man who remembered what it was like to be a boy, and it was with high spirits that we ran down through the orchard behind the old house to the new subdivision street to meet him. It was clear that the work day was well underway when we arrived. Uncle Dick met us and wasted no time in beginning our introduction to the world of paid employment. His first pronouncement was that, since we were working men now, the usual twenty-dollar stipend would be held until Friday. Our hours would be tallied, and if we had worked enough hours, the twenty each would be ours, if not we would be paid only the hours worked. Our money balloon was popped.

To his credit, he knew how to hold a juicy carrot before our innocent eyes. This carrot took the form of a 1949, very used, blue GMC pickup truck. He was actually going to let us kids take turns driving a real truck on the job! To a couple of boys our age, that was almost as good as getting paid.

The first task of the week was to take the truck down to the end of the street where there sat a towering heap of bricks that had been unloaded in the wrong location. Our job was to load the bricks into the truck, drive them to the further end of the street and stack them *neatly* for the masons to use on the current brick-home project.

Simple enough, but the truck was a floor shift, and neither of us kids had ever encountered this before. (I had driven the family Buick under my mother's supervision, but it was a non-shift, fluid-drive model, so that didn't count for much.)

Uncle Dick wasn't much help. "Figure it out for yourselves. It's an old piece of junk, so you can't hurt it, only don't leave this street."

He gave us the keys and a pair each of White Mule work gloves, the kind with leather palms, and pointed us toward the truck. I was elected to be the first driver because of my age and Buick experience. Off we jerked and bucked down the street to the pyramid of bricks. It was a big pile of bricks, a huge pile, in fact. We moved bricks for two hot, dusty, grimy never-ending days. The world of work quickly lost its glamour.

Wednesday morning, after a couple of hours of site cleanup, our slave-driver uncle pulled up in the old GMC pickup. "You boys look hot – how about I take you for a cold drink?" This sounded good to us, so we piled into the cab with him and headed out to the highway. After about a fifteen-minute jolly, joking ride, we slid into the gravel lot of an old wooden roadside store and gas station. "You boys run on in and get us some drinks and snacks while I gas up Old Blue here – tell Mr. Vines I'll pay up when I come in."

We enjoyed our break on a bench under the roof overhang on the shady side of the store, the side with the peeling Jefferson Island Salt advertisement. I had a big, long-neck bottle of RC Cola and package of fluffy pink snowball cakes. Patrick had some sort of orange soda and a bag of peanuts – ugh! Uncle Dick had a Nugrape Soda and a tin of potted meat and crackers. (Don't ask me to describe what potted meat is. It was so awful that it defied even kid taste – even mine, and I had been known to scarf down a can of slimy Vienna sausages in one sitting.)

Once our savory-snack time was over, we mounted the GMC relic and tottered down the highway. I don't know why we didn't question the direction or length of this outing or why there were two evil-looking, pointed shovels and some fishing gear in the truck bed.

After about another five minutes, we pulled off the highway just a few feet shy of a bridge abutment, next to a small but deep creek, adjoining a beautiful bank of white sand.

"O.K," Uncle Dick announced, "you boys hop out and grab those shovels. I want you to fill the truck bed up to just under the edge with that fine bank sand while I go upstream and catch a fish."

This simple-sounding order took about an hour and a half of hot, sandy work, all the while using our meager cursing vocabulary. I'm sure Dick could hear us from where he was fishing, and I'm equally sure he was thoroughly enjoying himself.

The rest of the week is a blur of menial construction-site tasks. At last, Friday afternoon arrived. Pay day at long last! The reckoning was presented in the shade of a half-finished basement. We had earned $18.50 each by Dick's count. However, there was yet another lesson to be learned that hot Friday evening. WE HAD TO PAY $1.25 EACH FOR THE WHITE MULE WORK GLOVES WE WORE OUT MOVING THOSE GAZILLION BRICKS! That left us $17.25 each, and raw, red hands.

It was a lesson we quickly absorbed. The next week, we pleaded with our grandfather to take us with him on a business trip to the state capital about three hours south. This turned out to be a blessing in three ways. First, it got us out of the construction business. Second, when we reached our destination, our grandfather put his hand in his pocket and pulled out a twenty for each of us. ("In case you boys need some extra spending money," he winked.) Third, I saw my first Marilyn Monroe movie!

Don't get the wrong idea about my uncle. He wanted to show us the real world. Other times, he let us ride behind him on his gigantic Harley and spend time in the "adults only" pool hall learning how to shoot complicated three-rail shots while being watched over by the day manager, a guy accurately named Greasy.

Dick was, and remains, my favorite uncle *but don't get in a truck with him*.

CHAPTER TWENTY-FIVE

OUTFISHING THE BIG GUYS

One of the signal triumphs of my early teenaged years occurred during that same summer's visit to our grandparents, for one of boyhood's biggest achievements was to best a grownup or a group of grownups in some field of endeavor, especially if they didn't want you involved.

Uncle Dick, who'd been a little peeved at my and Patrick's getting out of the construction-slave business, relented pretty quickly and invited us to go out next morning with him and a few of his friends for a day of fishing on a nearby lake on which he had some property. This prompted what seemed to us to be a brilliant idea – not only would we go fishing, but – once the day's fishing was done – Dick could leave us on the lakeshore overnight so we could camp out and fish on our own.

When told about this brainstorm, Dick – as usual when faced with that kind of kid idea – just grinned and said, "I don't see why not."

The next day began very early, as fishing expeditions usually do, but we didn't care. It was fun to be two kids among a group of cussing, beer-drinking and all-around fun men. Not that they exactly included us, but it was pretty good just to be up-close observers of what we already recognized as a genuinely male rite. It was a rite, moreover, that we hadn't been previously exposed to because we were city boys whose parents weren't into fishing, and Uncle Dick had never taken us on one of these all-male expeditions before.

My chance to shine came in the late afternoon. Uncle Dick and a couple of his friends were going out in the boat to troll for bass in another part of the lake. I begged to ride with them, while my cousin Patrick stayed behind, fishing off the dock with a cane pole and some crickets. As the boat reached the spot that the experienced fishermen thought was ripe and ready, the rods and reels were broken out and lures were carefully chosen. I soon realized that there was no rod for me.

When I pointed out this lack of equipment, I was told, "Just as well. You really don't know much about fishing. You'd probably just hook one of us or yourself."

Oh, great, I sighed to myself. I was just going to get to sit in the oily bilge water and watch the great fishermen troll for the big ones. After about an hour and a half, I began to get extremely bored. For one thing, I had absolutely nothing to do. For another, the big-time fishermen weren't having any luck. Zilch. Not so much as a nibble.

For want of anything better to do, I began to rummage through the various tackle boxes with an idea of, somehow, cobbling together a fishing rig of my own. After splicing together a few pieces of scrap lines, I attached an inch-and-a-half single hook, along with a couple of lead split shot. The only problem I had now was the lack of bait or lure. No one offered to provide me with what I needed, so I kept poking around. An old, white pocket handkerchief that I found in one of the boxes held possibilities, I thought. As the grown-ups watched in amusement, I tore a strip about one inch by six inches off the cloth and tied it to my hook. Still not being trusted with a rod or pole, I just tied my line to a gunwale cleat and fed it out into the wake of the boat.

After about twenty minutes, I checked my line – it seemed taut and strained. I began to pull it in, inch by inch, hooking the slacked line around the cleat.

"Hey," I yelled excitedly over the motor noise, "I've got something on my line. Hey! I'm not kidding!"

"Slow down, Carl," my uncle shouted to the helmsman. "The kid thinks he's caught something – probably just a snag."

Carl slowed the boat to an idle while I kept pulling my line on board. I could feel the line moving as I tugged it over the gunwale. My excitement grew. This wasn't just some snag or limb caught on my hook.

"I think the kid may have something on that line," the other guy said.

"I told you I did," I answered, continuing to tug. My uncle reluctantly reached for a landing net and moved over to my side of the boat. With one last heave on the line, I flipped in a small-mouth bass about eighteen inches in length.

"Hot damn! Look at that bass!" said Dick as he held up my catch. "What did you use for bait? I don't see a lure on the line."

"I didn't have a lure. You guys wouldn't give me one," I pointed out, "so I just used white cloth. See it on the side gill?"

"Damn, who would have thought you could catch a fish like that with practically nothing," grumbled my uncle.

Not much was said about my catch on the trip back to the dock. What could they say? They had been bested by a kid with a string. The kicker was that none of them had landed a fish the entire outing. A few were hooked, but got off or broke the line. I was the only fisherman in that boat who'd scored.

When we rejoined my cousin at the dock, my accomplishment was recognized when my uncle showed my catch to a couple of other fishermen. He even admitted that they had rotten luck and that my bass was all we brought back. The other fishermen looked at my fish and then at me in respectful acknowledgment.

As the day wore on, the preparations for my and Patrick's camp were being made. We had a two-man Army-surplus pup tent, some soft drinks, some canned beans, Brunswick stew, one iron pot, some plastic forks and plates, and half a loaf of bread – everything a boy needed for a few hours away from home. We also managed to talk my uncle into leaving some fishing gear – line, hooks, a bucket of minnows, and bobbers, which was good because we were planning on doing some serious night fishing. We played it cool as long as they were around, but our plan was to show up the big buys with our catch. At last the grownups got their trucks packed up and began to leave.

Uncle Dick walked back to our pile of camping gear. "O.K, boys, I'll be back for you about seven in the morning." Then, grinning, he left too.

The great adventure had begun!

Camping out always means building a fire. Luckily, we were

left with a book of matches (with a Vargas girl on the cover, no less). We gathered wood, set up the two-part tent and cut some poles to use with the line, hooks, minnows, and bobbers we'd been left with.

Everything was going exactly as planned, and we were having a great time. The first indication that the night might not *continue* to go as planned involved the supper preparations. Since we had only one pot, we decided to heat the stew first. I was designated to be the cook and quickly learned some basic culinary rules. Rule 1: You can't cook canned food without a can opener. Not a great start. There we were with a fire, pot, an unopened can of stew and a setting sun. The plastic forks were of no use, so we searched the dock area for some kind of tool with which to pry open the can of stew. Patrick found a bent and broken kitchen knife some fishermen had discarded. With this inadequate tool, we bashed our way into the stew and also the beans, but it was not a pretty sight.

Our messy, sooty supper set the tone for the rest of the night. About nine o'clock (that's a guess – we had no watch), the mosquitoes descended. At first we tried to ignore them. They were just a bunch of bugs, after all, but they finally got the best of us and we ran into the lake, splashing around in the murky water to get them off us. It helped momentarily, but when we came out the mosquitoes were waiting. Soon, an extremely bright moon eased over the trees and gave us plenty of light by which to suffer.

Our night-fishing project was forgotten in the mad fight against the insect world. We tried to button ourselves in the tent, but the heat soon drove us out. Finally, we took the tent down, separated the two halves, and then each rolled himself up in a half, attempting to create a protective cocoon. While not perfect, this worked better than the other bug-avoidance strategies we'd tried, and we somehow managed to fall asleep before dawn. Our breakfast consisted of limp loaf bread and warm orangeade. As promised, Uncle Dick returned to retrieve us. We were a sorry-looking lot – all dirty, spotted, hungry and awfully tired.

After he'd deposited our gear in his car's trunk and us in the backseat, he turned to us and said, "Well, boys, where's all those fish you were going to have this morning?"

Patrick grunted. "Still in the damn lake if you really want to know."

Dick laughed most of the way home. I think it was his revenge for my triumph of the day before. The next time he asked me to go fishing, I made sure I took my own pole.

CHAPTER TWENTY-SIX

A NAZI DAGGER SAVES THE DAY

W hen I graduated from elementary school at the end of May, the one worrying thought that I took away with me involved rumors of the hazing that we boys would have to endure once high school started in September. I didn't totally believe these tales of torture and intimidation. At the same time, I couldn't help thinking that there must be *something* to them, and the stories were pretty intense. Some freshmen boys were beaten, they said, others robbed of their allowances, and some even subjected to the humiliation of a plain, old-fashioned "pantsing." (The last may have bothered us most, because nobody wanted his pants and underpants removed in public view.) The more we passed these rumors around, of course, the wilder they became.

Once I was away from our old grade-school routine, however, facing a summer that lay before me like a never-ending, shimmering highway of promise, the rumors began to recede and quickly evaporated as I became distracted by a more-or-less continuous round of fun. I messed around with Vernon, modifying his Schwinn into the "motorized wonder." I went on a Scout campout. I flew my favorite model airplanes. I spent two weeks with my grandparents. I went on swimming parties, during one of which I met an awfully cute girl named Georgeanne whom I found myself thinking about a lot. And there were always bike rides and long afternoons spent playing never-

ending Monopoly games. In my *leisure time*, I worked on my model railroad and generally goofed around.

It was a good summer. Heck, it was a *great* summer. But even great summers must come to an end, and suddenly it was mid-August and my mother was taking me downtown to the teenage-boy section of her favorite department store to select clothes. I needed just about everything, for I'd had a growth spurt and was now taller than my six-foot-tall father.

"How you dress your first year in high school is very important," my mother proclaimed as we strolled the wide aisles, looking at clothing as the salesman extolled the virtues of first one thing, then another. He was especially keen to interest us in a leather jacket of the sort that looked a lot like the ones John Wayne had worn in all those World War II movies that I'd devoured over the years. I hinted and then stated that this was my preference of all the things we'd seen. For once, my mother paid no attention, and I ended up with a tame assortment of perfectly appropriate, boring gear, including a large stack of brand-new underwear so white it almost shone. We proceeded to the Shoe Department, in which she reluctantly let me choose a pair of Converse sneakers instead of the lace-up oxfords or saddle shoes she and the salesman favored.

It was the shopping trip that reactivated the memory of all those rumors. If Vernon had been around, I maybe could have gotten some information out of him because he'd started high school the semester before, but he and his mother were on their annual monthly visit to his grandparents on a farm in another county. I thought about calling him, but I didn't want to admit I was worried and calling *long distance* would have totally given it away. Anyway, I wasn't sure Vernon could be any help. The kids who started high school in January probably avoided some of the hassles almost certain to be visited on those of us who came in after a long summer undoubtedly used by the older boys to plot novel ways to torment us. Anyway, nobody much messed with Vernon because his reputation preceded him. He was quiet and usually kept to himself, but his temper was ferocious and well-known, as was his creativity with weapons of destruction, all of which kept him from easy-target status.

A few days before school was to start, I met up with Freddie, another incoming freshman, who lived on the next block, and we talked for a while about some of the things we'd heard back in May. On the spur of the moment, we decided to get on bikes and ride up to take a look at the place, which in a physical sense both of us knew very well. The grammar school we attended was only about two hundred yards away from the high school, and in between them were areas for sports, including the high-school football field whose wide-open spaces we often used for airplane and kite flying, bike riding, stunts, and rocket launching. No one had ever seemed to care about us younger kids using the high-school grounds as long as we didn't set the grass on fire. Not that - apart from said scraggly grass - there was a lot we could damage. The bleachers, which sat on the southern side of the field, were of concrete over a large earth berm, so were indestructible. They made a terrific launch pad for our aircraft and rockets.

So close together the two school buildings were, yet they occupied completely different and totally separate universes in our scheme of things. It didn't help that, when the grammar-school graduating class entered high school, they just disappeared inside the big red-brick building, never to be seen again. Vernon hadn't disappeared, of course, but Vernon was always an exception to everything, so I didn't count him. Anyway, he never talked about what went on in the sprawling high-school building, probably because he didn't notice.

The days seemed almost to melt away as fast as a Fudgsicle on a hot day. School was to start the day after Labor Day. My parents, as usual, invited some of the local relatives to our house for a holiday cookout. Among the guests were my Aunt Marge and my cousin Patrick, whom I hadn't seen since we'd returned from the visit to our grandparents a couple of months earlier. My mother invited Patrick to stay over for the night since he lived at the far end of the county and the two of us probably wouldn't see each other again until the winter holidays.

I don't remember whose idea it was, but – without saying anything to our parents – we slipped away and got out one of my father's war souvenirs, a Nazi dagger. All we planned to do was just to look at it. It was worth looking at. It had a sharp, blue, oiled-steel blade about twelve inches long, and there was a wicked-looking eagle head on the butt of the handle. I had seen this nasty bit of weaponry many times before and had even handled it, albeit with care, always putting it back in its sheath, to be immediately returned to the bureau drawer where it normally resided.

But this time Patrick and I started waving it about, never thinking about its length and sharpness. We were just goofing around and showing off, certainly not fighting, but somehow the tip of the blade was shoved into the right side of my nose, almost through to the other side.

My first feeling was that someone had punched me square in the face. I didn't realize I had been stabbed until my vision became red from the blood spurting from my almost-severed nose. I grabbed a towel and ran to the living room where the adults were sitting, mumbling something about maybe going to the hospital, which scared my mother half to death for I always resisted any suggestion I needed medical care for anything. The two-mile ride to the emergency room was scarier than the stabbing. For some reason, my mother was driving me herself, and in a hurry! I guess my father stayed home to yell at Patrick and put the dagger away for good (I never saw it again – I think he may have sold it).

The emergency-room treatment was thorough. After about two hours, five stitches and a lot of blood mopping, I was sent home with a very large bandage covering the right side of my face, eye and all. I couldn't even wear my glasses. Aunt Marge and Patrick were gone.

The next day was the dreaded Freshman Orientation at the high school. In spite of the pain of the injury, I woke up worrying about all the things that could happen on this horrible first day. I started to dress and got as far as my shirt when I *remembered*. Starting over, I put on one of the sets of new underwear, then redressed myself. My mother, still doing her hair and makeup, asked if I felt like walking or if I'd better wait and let her drive me on her way to work. I told her I was fine, which was sort of true. (I'll admit it crossed my mind to say I didn't feel like going, but I figured it was better just to go ahead and get whatever was going to happen over with.)

The high school was an easy four-block walk from home, but those blocks seemed like miles. I caught up with Freddie on the next street over. Explaining what was beneath the enormous bandage over part of my face took a couple of minutes, then we fell silent as we trudged toward the school, two relatively timid kids, to face our fate together. As we walked along the track next to the football field, our worst fears assumed human form. Two gigantic senior-football-player types appeared from behind the bleachers and stopped in our path. We froze in place. They stepped a few feet closer.

"You guys freshmen?" the larger one boomed?

GULP!

"Yeah," I said, tentatively.

"Well, you guys had better haul ass 'cause freshman orientation starts in a couple of minutes and the principal is a real mean son of a gun."

They continued on their way, leaving us breathless but untouched. Freddie said it was because of the bandage.

"They didn't bust our asses. It must have been 'cause they figured someone had already got to you."

Whatever the reason, we survived to live another day. Maybe the Nazi dagger did me a favor after all.

CHAPTER TWENTY-SEVEN

HIGH SCHOOL REALITIES

High school proved to be something of a letdown. I was relieved not to have been attacked or robbed or, especially, pantsed on my first day. At the same time, once the high-school principal welcomed us and they handed out our schedules, it didn't feel all that different from elementary school, in part because both schools had been built within a couple of years of each other, in the same red brick with the same tall windows, wooden floors, and high ceilings. The same kind of long hook-tipped poles leaned in the corners so that, as in elementary school, certain selected boys (usually the tallest, strongest and least clumsy) could open the large windows from the top, a necessity for good air flow on warm days.

True, the hallways were bigger and longer, the stairs wider, and the auditorium much larger, with a real stage, a balcony, and a floor that sloped gradually from the rear entrance doors toward the orchestra pit. Along with the limp vegetables, limper meats, runny Jell-o salads, and oversteamed rolls we'd come to know so well in elementary school, the lunchroom served a somewhat wider range of food actually appealing to kids, like hamburgers, hot dogs, and potato chips. We no longer moved as a class in lockstep, but went from room to room as individuals, making it easier to cut a class or at least shave a few minutes off the front of it as long as you had a halfway-decent excuse. The two-dozen kids with whom I'd gone through eight years of elemen-

tary school were joined by about 175 strangers from other schools in the high school's feeder area, and everybody began to regroup to some extent. Those of us who'd known one another forever remained friends, or at least friendly, but the wider range of activities available in high school drew everyone into a self-sorting process. Vernon was big into the Science Club because it gave him additional access to the school labs for experiments that were growing increasingly more technical and therefore less interesting to me. Several of my old neighborhood buddies donned sports uniforms and practiced by-the-book regulations – Jeff for baseball, Lee and Billy for football, Charles for basketball, Johnny for track, and Freddie for tennis. Some also went in for music – Jeff and Johnny joined the band, Lee the choir, and Richard the orchestra.

Tall and skinny and getting more so every day, not particularly interested in organized sports and equally unmusical, I drifted over to the Art Department, hidden on the ground floor behind the boiler room and equipment storage. There a small group of like-minded visual obsessives were holed up with a tolerant teacher, plenty of art supplies, and a kiln. All the way through school, I'd known other kids who were into art in a mild sort of way, but this was the first time I'd been around people my own age who, like me, always had a pad and pen or pencil or other material at hand and never stopped drawing, or painting, or sculpting. It was fun to see what they were doing and to show them what I could do. I especially enjoyed getting familiar with the kiln and playing around making pottery animals of loose form and fantastic surfaces. Art began to assume an even more important role in my life. It didn't hurt that there were some really cute girls in the classes – Doris, petite, with a cap of short, curly brown hair and a face like a kewpie doll; Margaret, cool and blonde, with intense blue eyes; Marie, dramatic looking and quirky; and Virginia, a classic beauty with auburn hair, big hazel eyes, and a scattering of freckles across her nose. All older than me, of course, but a fellow could dream.

Away from class, I made some new lunchroom friends – Don and Jimmy, who like me hated the school food. We'd pass on what was supposed to be good for us and fill up on junk while we sneakily eyed the pretty girls who usually sat at the next table, talking about the time in the (hopefully) not-too-distant future when we'd have our first real wheels.

My old neighborhood buddy Freddie and I checked out a couple of the school's football games, held at a very large stadium only a few miles away that was used in turn by all the area high schools on Thursday and Friday nights, as well as by a couple of nearby colleges on Saturday nights. The experiment was not a success. Our team was pathetic, almost always losing by embarrassing margins (a losing spread of less than thirty points was considered almost as good as a win). The band was worse, consisting as it did of only a couple of dozen players led by this strange-looking band director, their performance completely overwhelmed by the size of the stadium and the dozen majorettes that bounced around them on the field in calf-high boots, enormous military-style hats with plumes, mid-thigh pleated skirts and heavily ornamented vests over long-sleeved shirts. (We heard that one of the Majorette Mothers disapproved of anything more revealing as too immodest for young ladies.) The only area a pair of curious boys could ogle on those majorettes was from mid-calf to mid-thigh (great for the knee enthusiast), which on the nights we were on hand was blue with cold.

The only bright spot was the cheerleading squad, whose eleven members somehow managed to remain energetically sexy in spite of the inevitably depressing outcome of the game for the team they so valiantly cheered on.

I was especially interested in the cheerleading squad, for I knew the head cheerleader, Annette, known as Annie, the sister of Charles, one of my friends from up the street. Annie, who was three years older, had been around my whole life, and it had been funny to see her go from being a short tomboy I vaguely remembered, with messy fair hair and a grin too big for her face, to a petite, really pretty girl of the wholesome Doris Day sort, not necessarily the most gorgeous girl in school but, from all indications, easily the most popular. Not just the head cheerleader, Annie had done it all – both Honor

Societies, National and Junior; annual staff; class officer; class favorite; the official "Sweetheart" of the school; *and* most likely to succeed.

Annie was the girl everyone held up to the other girls as an example of how someone could be pretty, popular, accomplished, and smart. Which was why it was such a shock when the rumors started, late in the fall semester. *Annie was going to have a baby.* I didn't believe it at first because it just didn't sound like Annie. I mean, thanks to the neighborhood information vine, I understood about the birds and bees, even before the somewhat awkward talk my father and I had had the year before, but it had been my impression that "nice" girls stayed out of that kind of trouble. Annie was definitely a nice girl, the nicest, so it couldn't be true. But it was. I ran into Charles and he brought the whole mess up. The family was having a real snit fit. She'd been sneaking out to meet this much older guy, just out of the service, and back in college on the GI Bill. He was, Charles told me, a real creep, but now they were stuck with him, for Annie and the creep were set to be married the following week.

The story got even messier later, for it was school-system policy to send girls who were either married or pregnant to a special school so their bad example wouldn't influence the other girls. (Actually, what the snotty girls' counselor said, Charles told me, was "contaminate," which was startling. One stupid mistake and Annie had gone from being the school golden girl to a source of contamination.)

Annie's family, however angry they might be, was not willing to see Annie exiled from the scene of all her triumphs just months away from graduation, and they got a lawyer, apparently a good one. After being absent for a couple of weeks, Annie was once again in school, "beginning to show," as the teachers whispered, but there was no further talk of sending her away. The next few months, there was an Annie pool around school: which would arrive first, Annie's kid or graduation? In the end, graduation won, but just barely. Annie graduated one week and had her baby the next.

It was my first exposure to the double standard. Boys who got girls pregnant were "spoken to," but that was all. There was never any talk of sending them away. This made no sense to me, and I actually tried to ask my parents about it, but they weren't interested. Annie was a wonderful girl in many ways, they said, but she had made a bad mistake and now was having to pay for it and that was that.

Apart from this example of society's disdain for one of its former favorites, high school continued for me much as had elementary school. I made mostly B's without too much work, with even one or two A's. (The book-report covers could still work their magic.) I managed to sit next to pretty girls in most of my classes, but never got up the nerve to talk to them. I kept attending Scout meetings and even the occasional campout. The biggest difference was that I began to think non-stop about cars.

CHAPTER TWENTY-EIGHT

HIGHWAY MUSIC

At last, school was out, the suspense of when Annie – the golden girl turned bad influence – would have her baby was ended by the great event itself, and I was at something of a loose end. None of my usual summertime pursuits seemed to be materializing. All the guys were either somewhere or other on vacation or working summertime jobs.

I had a low-key job myself, filling in for a kid up the way named Tommy, who paid me a daily rate to deliver papers to his large route when he couldn't. This suited me fine. I'd already memorized his route, so I always knew what needed to go where. I didn't have to make those hellish collection calls or keep up with money, both of which onerous chores had led to my relinquishing my own much smaller route a couple of years before. Still, Tommy didn't call on me a lot, and I was spending most of my time working on my HO-gauge railroad layout. One day I got bored and made the mistake of mentioning this fact to my father.

"I can fix that," he grinned.

His idea of "fixing" it was to give me a job at the large commercial laundry where he was the route supervisor. The laundry, one of the biggest in the city, offered home-pickup and -delivery services. Because there was a lot of competition, it was essential to maintain the expected routes on the days promised; and one of my father's key responsibilities as route supervisor was to make sure that this was done. Unfortunately, the dozen or so people who worked delivery had the unfortunate habit of occasionally calling in sick, taking vacation time, or interfering in some other way with the smooth operation of the schedule he'd so carefully laid out.

My father's solution was to seek out a former employee who'd retired for health reasons to see if he would be willing to drive a route if he had some "legs" to do the climbing up and down steps, carrying packages of clean laundry and hangers of dry cleaning, and then hauling the load of dirty clothing and linens back to the van. It was me, of course, that my father intended to be the "legs" in this operation. His idea made sense. I had nothing particular to do, and I had several weeks before I was due to make the annual visit to my grandparents. Moreover, I was an energetic fifteen-year-old inexperienced enough to be willing to "run his butt off" for fifty cents an hour.

That was an interesting several weeks. Most of the routes we worked were in an extremely hilly part of town, with lots of multistory apartment houses without elevators. Still, the really hard part was not the physical exercise, but the hours. The work day began at 6:30 A.M., and I had to get up at 5:30 to go in with my father. This was a distinct contrast to my usual summer rising hour of 9:30 or ten. Hard or not, however, I worked as "legs" until it was time for the grandparent visit. Some of the money that I made I spent, but most of it I put in my savings account, where – already looking ahead to the fact that I would be old enough to get a car in just a few months – I'd been stockpiling income I'd earned for some time.

When the day for departure to visit my grandparents finally arrived, I got on the bus and was immediately struck by how strange it seemed to be traveling alone. My cousin Patrick, who usually accompanied me, was heavily involved in some sort of baseball league which, to my surprise, he valued more than these two weeks of unfettered and well-subsidized freedom. I was met at the bus station by my Aunt Gloria, the youngest of my mother's siblings, only a couple of years older than me and the only one of my grandparents' children still living at home.

On arrival at the house, I was given the first perk of the trip – my own room. Usually, my cousin and I had to share a bed located in what was basically a large back hallway in the old house. This arrangement, while hardly cramped given the size of the space, had the disadvantage of affording no privacy, especially from each other. Having the space to myself was a real step up. Maybe they were seeing me as more grownup given that I had turned fifteen in early June.

There were only a few rules at my grandparents' house. Rule One: Don't slam the front door (a wide, paneled-wood affair with an etched-glass upper half and stained-glass sidelights). Rule Two: DO NOT make any noise between 12:30 and 1 P.M. (My grandfather, once the hog futures had been announced on the radio, was in the habit of taking an after-lunch nap before returning to his office.) Rule Three: Don't eat the green pears from the trees by the front gate, as they are for canning only. (This rule had been instituted about four years earlier after an unfortunate stomach-pumping incident that I didn't like thinking about.)

I lay in bed that first night, luxuriating in the silence, thinking about the fact that, save for these minimal constraints, the next two weeks were mine. It would have felt good at any time, but after the weeks I'd spent working at the laundry, this was paradise. I went to sleep thinking about all the things I was going to do, none of which came anywhere near the rules.

The next day (Saturday), Gloria took me aside on the front porch. She whispered, "Can you keep a secret? I know Patrick couldn't, but I feel I can trust you."

Wow! Secrets already! This was definitely going to be a different summer.

"Sure," I said, dying to hear what she was going to confide.

"Daddy won't let me date this guy – you don't know him – so I've got to sneak out somehow to see him," she said. "What I want you to do is ask if someone will take you skating out at the rink on Highway 9 tonight, and I'll volunteer to do it."

I agreed, and during supper she poked me under the table to remind me to whine about skating. The request sounded normal, and Gloria piped up after a short pause and said, "I'll take him. I haven't used my skates in ages. It'll be fun."

About half an hour later, we were on our six-mile jaunt, me to skate, she to *whatever*. I was told that she would be back to pick me up at 10 P.M. when the rink closed. (Yeah, right.) I skated and skated, but it wasn't fun. I discovered that just rolling about a strange rink without anyone to fool around with or show off for had no appeal.

Ten P.M. came, and went. Every one was hustled out. Lights were turned off. The parking lot emptied. I was paying for my mendacity. No Gloria, no watch, no light, and no food (the last perhaps the most important for a teenaged boy with an unquenchable appetite). I had lots of time to think about how little fun I'd had and to vow that there would be no more solitary skating.

It was very dark, and very quiet. It turned out that, once the rink closed, almost no traffic came in that direction. I was beginning to wonder seriously what I should do next – I didn't, after all, want to get Gloria in trouble, but this was getting spooky – when she finally showed up, very apologetic and embarrassed.

On the way home, later than we'd said we'd be (it was after eleven), she promised me treats galore if I just played along with her alibi. The story was to be that, after a wonderful evening of skating, she and I went to the drive-in frequented by the college crowd and lost track of time as we stuffed ourselves with burgers, fries, and all sorts of ice-cream delights. I agreed. As it turned out, no one even knew when we got home. The best part of the whole charade was that the next evening she did treat me to a gut-stretching meal at the drive-in.

On Monday, my grandfather wanted to take me downtown to see his new office situated on the town square facing the courthouse. This was my second ride in his new Mercury sedan. You know that new-car smell – I was totally hooked on it. Later that day, after I had made the rounds of the downtown stores and tanked up on cheap orangeade at one of the drugstores, I was invited to take a drive with my grandfather to look at a property he was thinking about buying. On the highway out of town, I tentatively asked him if I could maybe drive the car. Being the kindly sort of grandpa, he said since I was almost sixteen (well, in eleven months) that he didn't see why not. We pulled over and swapped sides. I was allowed to drive for about fifteen minutes until we reached the property. My driving was evidently OK – he seemed to remain calm. I told him that my mother had been letting me drive her around in our huge old Buick and I had logged maybe eight hours behind the wheel.

Things went on as usual the next couple of days. At breakfast on Friday, my grandfather asked if I would do him a favor.

"Sure," I said. "I'll do anything for you." And meant it.

"Do you remember where the Taylor farm is, the place we went to on Monday?" he asked.

"Sure, just go out past the college on Route 12 till the river bridge and turn left," I answered.

"Well, I want you to take me to the office, pick up some papers and take them to Mr. Taylor," he said.

I was confused, and then hopeful. Did he actually want me to drive him downtown and then continue on a business delivery, alone? YES!

This was it. My first solo drive and in a brand new car! Life doesn't get sweeter.

My grandfather came through and, the package of papers in hand, I was given the car keys and an admonition to "be extra careful."

Easing the big green Mercury out of an angled parking space, I began my virgin solo drive. Getting out of town was nerve-wracking – so many lights and signs to watch out for. Once on the highway, however, with a good forty-five-minute round trip ahead of me, I began to get really excited. I was on my own for the first time – and in a new car. (I know I keep repeating that, but that's the way it felt.) I knew he was an indulgent grandfather, but I could not believe he let me have the car all alone. If Patrick ever found out about this, he'd be mad enough to spit.

It was a perfect summer day. With all the windows rolled down and the radio volume cranked up, I was in automotive heaven. That's when the ultimate moment happened. *Maybellene* came on the radio. Driving along, the wind blowing across my crewcut, the radio at full blast, I mainlined the insistent beat, "motivatin over the hill" right along with Chuck Berry's description of *his* highway experience.

That's when I heard the highway sound.

And I could hear it too, that highway sound. Wow. There wasn't a Coupe de Ville in sight, and I was in a Mercury not a Ford, but Chuck was singing to *me*. I might not be mourning Maybellene's lost virtue, but this was my road and my time.

The moment was complete when I had to stop at a crossroads and two pretty college-age girls in a '55 Bel Air convertible turned onto the highway in front of me, waving as they went by. Wow. Older girls. Waving. *At me*. What could be sweeter?

What else can I say? The package was delivered, the return trip was uneventful, and the car was put (carefully) into a parking space near the office.

When I reported in, my grandfather asked, looking up from his desk, "Well, Bobby, how did the car perform? Was Mr. Taylor at home?"

"Yes sir, he was there, and the car is wonderful," I replied.

"Gloria thought you might like to take a spin on your own," he replied, grinning.

"Gloria?" I was surprised. What did she have to do with this? Then it hit me. She had worked on her father to let me drive his car as part of the payback for keeping her secret. What an aunt.

CHAPTER TWENTY-NINE

THE SODA JERK SAGA

Sophomore year was pretty much a repeat of being a freshman. I endured all the classes, except for art, which I continued to enjoy. I rediscovered a girl on whom I'd had a crush years before, but I still couldn't decide if I liked her well enough to risk a serious approach. Don, Jimmy and I continued to sit together at lunch and eye the pretty, giggling girls at the next table as we discussed vehicle possibilities. Freddie and I gave the school football games another shot before deciding the experience was too embarrassing to be worth the trouble, even for the possibility of meeting girls. I filled in for Tommy on his big paper route whenever he was out of town demonstrating experiments at various science fairs. Vernon and I still checked in with each other pretty regularly, but our interests were already taking us in very different directions, me to an expansion of my art obsession, him to some fairly heavy-duty high-school science. My HO-gauge layout remained relegated to my bedroom so my parents could turn the sunroom into a TV-viewing lounge. I enjoyed working on the layout weekends, but not all the time and not every weekend. I kept up with the Scout meetings, continuing to bike the few blocks as the days grew shorter, still stopping by Charlie's for a hamburger and Chocolate Soldier. We had a pretty good campout that fall. A couple of the boys in our troop were going for Eagle, and I picked up some additional merit badges. On Saturdays I still tanked up on my loaf-of-French-bread-and-chocolate-milk diet. Yet, in spite of the fact that a lot of my life was much as it had been, things started feeling different somehow. Maybe it was that guys I'd once seen every day were no longer a part of my routine, maybe it was just that I was beginning to grow up, not only in size but in other ways I couldn't define. I couldn't quite put my finger on it, but everything seemed to be changing in some subtle way.

That Christmas, when asked what I wanted by my parents and grandparents, I said what I'd really like was money to put into my car account, which continued to grow, but not fast enough it seemed to me. Save for a couple of token items – a record album and a jacket my mother knew I especially wanted – they listened, and instead of having the usual pile of brightly wrapped packages to rip into, I was confronted on Christmas morning by paper gift wallets containing checks with the words "Your car" written in the "For" space. I should have been pleased, but it suddenly felt *wrong* not to have any fun stuff.

Once the holidays were over, we were back in school and the days seemed to stretch endlessly toward summer, the special summer of 1956 when I'd at last be old enough to get a car. I became obsessed with anything automotive. I pored over magazines, biked to car lots, read the car section of the classifieds, stayed in my seat when car commercials came on TV, and swiveled so often to look at passing cars of interest whenever we were driving anywhere that my father said it made him dizzy to watch.

He teased me a lot about how much I wanted a car. Still, it was because of my father that the perfect car turned up and because of my parents that I was able to buy it. In spite of saving just about everything I'd earned in the last year and the gift money I'd been given, I had only a little more than three hundred dollars stashed away in my "car" fund, not nearly enough for a decent car, even in 1956. My father knew this and said he and my mother would help me out if I liked the car he'd located, a cute blue 1951 Ford convertible, or – as I came to think of it – the Humility Machine, about which you'll hear more later.

The car cost six hundred and fifty dollars. My father didn't dwell on the fact that the three hundred and twenty-five dollars he and my mother had chipped in for the convertible's purchase could be viewed, at least in part, as a loan, but I got the drift. He wouldn't object if I repaid a little of it every once in a while. Then, there was the matter of insurance. The car was covered under our existing family policy, but my being just sixteen bumped up the rate, so part of my agreement with my father was that I was to help cover some of the premium increase. Then, there was the cost of the title and tag. Then, there were the operating expenses. Gas and repairs were to be my responsibility.

It became immediately apparent to me that I needed a job, ASAP, and not just filling in on another guy's paper route, however large. I did start looking, but hadn't made much headway when, after a few days, my mother came home with the news of a position she had secured for me. (I think she was looking more assiduously than I was! My parents, although admittedly on the indulgent side, were nonetheless firm believers in kids having jobs, as a character-building exercise if nothing else.)

I was informed by my mother that the job was not just any job, but one that most kids would die for. "A dream job," she assured me.

I was to be a soda jerk. The words were no sooner out of her mouth than I had a visual image of myself as the producer of wonderful, foamy, dreamy ice-cream treats covered in rich chocolate sauces and topped with juicy, shiny, long-stem cherries.

This sounded good to me. I was familiar with soda fountains, not only as a customer, but also as an avid consumer of magazines and movies. According to these media, soda fountains were always crowded with teenagers, mostly girls, leaning over the immaculately gleaming chrome-and-white array of dispensers of delights, focused on the attendant (me!), the center of attention, all eyes on his masterful handling of these complicated fountain concoctions. Ah, what a glorious image. I was ready to start immediately, which was a good thing because the car expenses sure had.

The Medical Point Pharmacy was located on the south side of downtown, about four miles from home, on the street level of a multi-story medical building where my mother worked at the time. She, knowing practically every one in the building, had talked the owner, Dr. Romano, into giving me the evening shift. I would work from four P.M. until 9:30 P.M., five days a week. Starting pay was seventy-five cents per hour.

The job orientation began on a Wednesday about 2 P.M. I

was told to come in early to meet the daytime staff. The soda fountain's day crew consisted of two nice, seemingly tidy, middle-aged ladies who had been working there for years. No one mentioned why the late-shift position was open. I, being wet behind the ears, never asked about my predecessor and really never heard who he or she was and where they went.

The orientation was a real kick in the gut. Yes, I would produce fountain treats, *but* I would also have to make sandwiches, serve canned soups, make and serve coffee, dispense Cokes, and cut pies.

Then came the killer. I WAS THE CLEAN-UP GUY. The wonderful chrome-and-white dispensers, the black-marble counter, the chrome back wall, and all vertical and horizontal surfaces of the approximately twenty-six-foot-long area were to be scrubbed, polished, and disinfected each and every night before I could go home.

The Norman Rockwell image in my head was fading fast. The worst part of these revelations was that this counter did a very brisk lunch trade, what with all the nearby offices and walk-in traffic. The NICE, TIDY ladies of the day shift didn't have time to clean, only to prepare and serve. From the looks of it, it seemed to me that they served most of the food and drinks to the floor, walls and appliances.

Well, a job is a job, especially when your financial need is urgent, so I paid attention when I was shown the basic layout of the work area and given general, very rudimentary instructions on how the soup-heating gizmo worked and where the cleaning rags, polish, mops, and Pinesol were located. Thank goodness I didn't have to learn or use the cash register – at the times I was there only the main register operated. When I served someone, I would write out a ticket, which the customer took to this main register, located at the pharmacy desk in the rear of the store.

What made the maintenance part of my job particularly difficult was that teenaged boys are not inclined to clean anything, except their cars, and I was no exception. The first two days were nothing but wiping, polishing, scrubbing and occasionally screwing up an order. Dr. Romano took the time to supervise my progress personally. I guess he wanted to keep the city health inspector happy, for he was very thorough in his nightly rounds.

The second tier of inspection was the day shift. They were relentless in their critique of my nightly labors. The worst job in my estimation was cleaning the behind-the-counter floor and duck-boards. Duckboards were slatted wooden walkways that covered the concrete floor. They kept the workers' feet out of the slime that collected during the day's frantic food fight. My last job of the evening was to remove the duckboards (they came in six-foot sections) to the alley in back, hose them down with hot water and Pinesol cleaner, leave them draining, then return to the fountain to scrape up the redolent goo that had collected during the last twenty-four hours. Then Pinesol was again scrubbed on the floor and hosed down a drain. Then the duckboards would be put back in place, ready for use.

However, let me bring up the BEST thing about this job, the food perk. I had an evening meal break, at which I was allowed to eat whatever I wanted. This was my chance to make up for the

pungent Pinesol punishment. My favorite concoction was just a chocolate malt, but made my way. The standard mix was two scoops of vanilla ice cream, two shots of chocolate syrup, a spoon of malt, and a cup of milk. My formula was more generous. First, I took the big chrome mixing can, crammed it full of chocolate ice cream, filled any left-over space with milk, malt and (instead of chocolate syrup) hot fudge from the ever-cooking pot normally reserved for hot-fudge sundaes. The most trouble with this delight was getting it onto the big green-and-chrome Hamilton Beach quad mixer. My concoction was so thick that the mixing blade could hardly penetrate the semisolid delight. But it could be done. This malt, plus a can of Campbell tomato soup and some sort of sandwich would last me until about 9 P.M.

My nightcap before tackling the duckboards was a double cherry Coke, also mixed to my recipe. This refreshing beverage was simple to make. From the cherry syrup pump, I'd put two long pumps into a twelve-ounce coke glass followed by Coca-Cola from the fountain dispenser, which was usually weighted a little on the syrup side. (The normal formula was one-half pump of cherry with the Coke.)

There was another difference between my expectations and the reality of the Medical Point Pharmacy's soda fountain. There were no giggling girls or admiring boys. This was very much a daytime-business area, and the night shift was usually quiet, with only an occasional shopper having a Coke while waiting for a prescription to be filled. After a while, this suited me fine. I hated to have a customer after 8:30. The worst of the cleaning had been done, and I didn't want to dirty up anything for a latecomer.

You never knew what a latecomer might want, and it wasn't always what you expected. About eight o'clock one evening, a guy came in and wandered nervously around the aisles for a few minutes. Finally, he took a stool at my counter and ordered a Coke (great, no clean up). Shifting his gaze back and forth from me to the prescription counter, he leaned over to me and asked if I could get him some rubbers. I told him that they were under the counter in the pharmacy area and I was not allowed back there. I said, "You'll have to ask the pharmacist for them." Then it hit me. Jerelyn was on duty that night. She was the only female pharmacist I had ever seen, so I suppose there weren't too many in 1956. Dr. Romano was in his office in the rear, but we had firm instructions not to interrupt him while he was doing bookkeeping.

I felt a wave of embarrassment flood over both me and this lovestruck chicken.

"Can't you go and ask her for them?" the now red-faced customer whispered.

Reluctantly, and just as red-faced, I shuffled back to the rear counter and relayed his request to Jerelyn.

"Wow, you tell that big brave man if he wants them he can ask for them himself or get out," she said, rather loudly I thought.

As I turned back to my area, I saw the customer disappearing out the front door. Crap, I thought, he didn't pay for his Coke. Reaching the counter where he'd sat, I found a crisp dollar bill, 20 cents for his Coke, the rest – I guessed – for his embarrassment.

My three months on this job ended in late August, when - somewhat later than usual - I made the annual trek to visit my grandparents. In spite of my special malts, I was ready to go. As far as I was concerned, it was a long-enough time for the soda-fountain life. Still, I did learn one lesson that summer: beware of anything described as "a dream job" and accept that dreams can turn into Pinesol nightmares.

CHAPTER THIRTY

THE HUMILITY MACHINE.

Ah, The Humility Machine, what a sweetie it was, even though the relationship began ambiguously. Let me backtrack a little and explain how we met. When my father mentioned seeing a car he thought I'd like and that, if I liked it, he and my mother would help me out with its cost, I was thrilled. It was after I'd gone to bed that night that the apprehension set in. What kind of car would my *father*, who drove a Buick Roadmaster, come up with?

I should have remembered the album photographs of him with the cars of his youth, all sporty convertibles. If I had, I wouldn't have been surprised when, the next day, he turned up with a 1951 Ford convertible. It was cute. That always sounds inadequate as a description of a machine that is essentially no more than a capacity for brute movement encapsulated in enough steel to protect its innards, but in this instance it was accurate. The car was *cute*. It was light blue with a white convertible top. It had red-and-white seat covers. It had

fender skirts. It had everything an about-to-be-sixteen-year-old boy could want. I almost drooled as I inspected its many delights. Arrangements were made the next day for the purchase. My hard earned savings plus another three hundred and twenty-five dollars from my parents (sort of a loan) sealed the deal.

Our getting acquainted period was sweet, but brief. The immediate order of business, of course, was to show off the convertible to my friends. This meant putting the top down and loading up some car-hungry boys for a ride. That's when the car – which I quickly came to think of as The Humility Machine – gave me the first clue to what lay ahead: the top-raising and -lowering machinery didn't work. You had to unlatch the top from the windshield frame, push up, jump into the backseat, keep pushing the top up to a vertical stance, then lower it by hand, and gravity, down to its retracted position. All in all, not a good beginning. (To raise the top you had to follow the same steps in reverse.)

In spite of the top business, the blue convertible was a hit with the other guys, who were always willing to come along anywhere, which worked out pretty well for me. One good thing about keeping some riders with you was that the raising and lowering of the top was quicker and easier with help.

On weekends, I drove everywhere. All my parents had to do was to start to say that an errand needed running, and I was behind the wheel of my little blue beauty before the last words of the sentence were out of their mouths. I even drove to the occasional Scout meetings that my work schedule allowed me to attend. After the Scout meeting, a couple of the guys and I would head over to one of the local drive-ins for hot dogs and a milk shake. I enjoyed that car to the hilt, in every way I could. Which was good, because pain accompanied every pleasure.

So, there I was, a just-turned-sixteen-year-old with a car that was envy of everyone who mattered. *I had a car.* It was easily the love of my life to that point, but, like so many of life's loves, it quickly became a cruel and heartless taskmaster.

First there was the matter of money. Simply possessing this

vehicle, with the normal costs related to car ownership, meant that my carefree days of summer were over. I had to get a job, and so I became a soda jerk. This cut significantly into my free time for actually using the car, but it was fun to think of it as I made Cherry Cokes and scrubbed all the surfaces of the soda fountain with the dreaded Pinesol.

Then, in addition to these normal auto-related expenses, there was the seemingly endless stream of repairs. Throughout the summer – and continuing for the entire time I owned the convertible – unexpected vehicle issues occurred with surprising frequency: backfires when the engine was started in the rain, random pinging, a funny ticking noise accompanied by an unsettling flickering of the oil gauge, brake squealing, engine sputtering, and other noises I couldn't quite put a name to. From time to time, the car would buck as it clunked, as if it were a living thing and I'd offended it in some way. And the days the engine wasn't running roughly were fewer than those when it was.

Confronted with this kind of situation in relation to his new car with which he is still in the throes of first love, a guy goes one of two directions. He becomes an amateur mechanic, or he finds a professional mechanic willing to be creative without charging him an arm and a leg. Apart from a few relatively simple repairs that my more mechanically minded friends could help with, I did the latter, taking the convertible to Jocko, the same mechanic my father used, whenever I had a couple of bucks scraped together. This patient soul operated out of a corrugated metal building in a light-industrial area a couple of miles away. When I'd roll in, he'd listen gravely to whatever the current issue was, take a look, and make a diagnosis. I'd ask him tentatively what it would cost. He'd tell me, and sometimes, once I'd got my breath back, I'd be able to come up with the money on the spot and hang around until he was done. Other times, I'd have to make the car limp home to wait until I could accumulate enough to do what was needed. This wasn't fun stuff (I never had any illusions about being able to afford to repair the malfunctioning convertible top), but mundane things like brake shoes, an oil pump, a distributor cap, spark plugs, the voltage regulator, even a solenoid replacement. The car seemed to have some kind of weird instinct for when I had money in my pocket, at which time it would promptly develop a problem that cost just a few dollars more than I had on hand. It was very discouraging, but I loved my little blue beauty in spite of everything.

I was scheduled to work the soda-jerk job until mid-August when I would make the annual trip to visit my grandparents. I wanted to drive the convertible, of course, but my parents put their foot down. The convertible was OK around town, but a 200-mile trip was out of the question. I protested, but in my heart of hearts, I knew they were right and was even secretly relieved.

Once again, I rode the bus, again alone. It had been two years since my cousin Patrick and I had made the trip together, so it didn't seem so strange this time to be on my own. Again, my Aunt Gloria met me, and we stopped for a malt on the way home. She was full of all the news since my last visit, and everything looked just the same. It felt good to be back in that place that never seemed to change, like a real homecoming. I enjoyed the routine even more than usual if that was possible. I slept late, messed around the house with my grandmother and great aunt, and walked up to my grandfather's office on the courthouse square and then rode back with him to the house for lunch, at which the food was always plain but good. I liked the dining room in which we ate it, which was long and relatively narrow with a bank of tall windows on one side overlooking the backyard that sloped down a hill to the area, just out of sight, where my grandfather and Uncle Dick continued to build houses. After lunch and my grandfather's brief nap, he'd go back to his office. Sometimes I'd go with him and mess around the square for a few hours. Other times, I'd cadge the loan of a car and go out on the highway to the pool hall he owned. Once or twice I went out to the lake with Uncle Dick and his buddies and fished from the pier. A couple of times I even worked a little on the construction site with Dick.

In no time at all, the visit was over, and Dick was taking me back to the bus station.

"Now you be good," he winked as usual as he deposited me and my bag on the pavement next to the waiting bus. I didn't know about being good, but I sure knew I intended to be mobile. I was returning to my car!

When I got home, it was time for school to start, along with my new job, weekends only, as a bag boy at a nearby A&P grocery store. My father, who'd worked for years as the manager of various A&Ps, had called a buddy on my behalf. The bag-boy job paid seventy-five cents an hour – wow, big money – plus tips! This was pretty good – I knew other boys working worse jobs for less money. The hours fit my school schedule. I was to work Fridays from five P.M. until 9:30. Saturdays, I came in at eight A.M. and worked until 9:30 P.M. Sundays, the store was closed to the public, but about once a month I had to go in on Sunday afternoons to sweep, mop and wax the floors in the public areas of the store. Everybody but the female checkout clerks helped with this. Mr. Nally, the store manager, showed up to supervise and approve the end result. He was a firm, but fair, boss. We bag boys were a jolly crew, and he tolerated our clowning around and joking on cleanup day when it was just us. When the store was open, however, we were expected to be appropriately businesslike in front of customers.

My regular, non-Sunday job responsibilities called for me to work in the store where needed – mostly at the front, bagging groceries at one of the checkout stands, but sometimes arranging deliveries in the warehouse or stocking shelves in the store and even cleaning up spills. Each bag boy was assigned to one checkout clerk exclusively. Mine was Vera, a very nice, divorced single mother. We made a good team, working in a smooth rhythm. At the end of the day – unlike some of the other checkout clerks – Vera, a good sport, was happy to take my tip change, count it, and convert it to "folding money" to save my pockets. On a good Friday night, the weight of the coins I'd accumulate was capable of ripping out all but the strongest seams.

Mr. Nally ran a tight ship. When hired, we bag boys were given strict instructions on how to treat customers. Always be courteous, friendly, helpful and neat. (We wore white A&P aprons and were to change them when they became the least bit soiled.)

The bag-boy job was pretty lucrative as well as eye-opening. I could make as much as $25 in tips on a good weekend, and observing the way in which people tipped was an important life lesson for me.

The car that was the reason for my introduction into the world of regular employment, my sweet blue convertible, even seemed to know about those good weekends. The second I got more than $25 together, The Humility Machine would need a repair that cost $30. My father said it beat anything he'd ever seen; it was, he would continue, as if that car had a crystal ball. Somehow I managed to keep it rolling, which was good because it was about to become the chariot that would carry me into a new stage of my life, one that – at long last – involved girls, up close and personal.

CHAPTER THIRTY-ONE

2-8-2 OR HOW MODEL RAILROADING IMPROVED MY LOVE LIFE

Having a car definitely made a difference when it came to girls. You suddenly became noticeable, though not always for the reason you wanted. One Monday, while driving through the neighborhood, top down, I saw two girls from school on the corner of the next block, within a couple of doors of being home. I knew there was no point in offering them a ride. Still, I thought I would cruise by, looking good, and give them a wave – hey, you never knew what could come of a simple courteous gesture.

As I passed them, I threw The Humility Machine's gear shift into second. CLUNK! Something broke underneath. As I continued on, another clanging sound erupted. I looked back and saw my drive shaft lying in the street. Since I was rolling downhill and the girls were still in sight, I decided to fake it and roll on, with no power. Once out of sight of the girls, I parked the car and hiked about four blocks to my friend Tubby's house. He had a rattle-bones Plymouth his father had come up with, and I hoped it would be able to tow me home. He said he thought it would, so we retrieved my drive shaft, then pulled my baby-blue heartache home for repairs. We then went to the parts store for a new rear universal joint. Nineteen dollars and twenty-six cents. That surprised me, for it broke the usual pattern that the convertible and I had jointly established, in which I earned money and the car required it, all of it, more than all of it, in fact. I'd had a super-good weekend at the A&P and had twenty-three dollars in my pocket. I'd put one over on the car! I had three dollars and seventy-four cents left. My glee didn't last long. Tubby wanted one dollar for gas and another for wear and tear on his aged Plymouth, which left me with exactly one dollar and seventy-four cents to last me the entire week. Whoopee!

I had become very aware of girls, in particular of a certain girl, thanks to Mr. Bauman's chemistry class. On the first day, I was a little early and took a seat beside Linda, a girl I'd known since second grade, who was even earlier. She smiled politely and turned her attention back to the book she was reading. Others began to drift in, including Mr. Bauman, a dapper, short man in crisply pressed pants and a white lab coat, under which he wore a neatly buttoned-up white dress shirt and bright-red tie. Class began, and Mr. Bauman began to outline what we were going to cover that term. I sort of listened, but I found my eyes drifting to my left, where Linda sat, seemingly totally absorbed, even though I couldn't help noticing she was doodling the whole time. I was surprised by her a little bit. It wasn't so much that she looked all that different – she'd always been pretty – but now her curly hair was pulled back into a tidy pony tail, she wore lipstick, and her knees – perpetually scabby throughout our childhood – seemed to have healed just fine. I began to develop my strategy.

We'd always been on speaking terms in various classes, but I'd never even thought about asking her out because I had a crush on a girl named Nancy and Linda seemed to have a thing going with another member of the band. Now, Nancy receding to the back of my mind, I not only wanted to ask Linda out; I wanted her to accept. I had to be sure to get it right the first time. I plotted and planned the hows and whens for a couple of weeks. It helped that she and I shared a lab table and the assigned experiments, which forced us to become even better acquainted. (Strengthening our growing bond was the fact that I was the one who ran for the school nurse when she absentmindedly let nitric acid we were diluting drip onto the back of her hand.) She was never anything but friendly, but for some reason getting up the nerve to pop the date question was requiring a super-

human effort in spite of the fact that I could tell she liked me. I couldn't figure out why getting the words out was such a problem. There was no reason I shouldn't ask her out, and not any reason for her to refuse. I now had a car of my own and a job that provided enough money for a reasonable level of entertainment. If I was ever going to get up the nerve to do it, I realized, I was just going to have to do it.

She was a member of the school band, so I figured she might need a ride to the football game Friday night and maybe an evening out afterwards. My invitation was not exactly a thing of beauty, but *she accepted*! Wow, what a relief. We set a time (I knew where she lived), and I got her phone number. Now it was time to get the car washed and waxed, my crew cut trimmed up, and my wardrobe selected. The one thing I didn't prepare for – because I didn't know I needed to – was the *father* interrogation to come. (I guess I should have compared notes with some of the other boys who'd made it to her front door.)

I arrived at six o'clock – blissfully unaware of what lay ahead – to collect Linda and her French horn. The game didn't start until 7:30, but I wanted to be sure we had plenty of time to meet up with the band before game time. I was, of course, nervous because it was a first date, and some anxiety was natural if you were a sixteen-year-old calling for a smashing girl from chemistry class. It was just as well that I didn't know what was waiting for me inside, or I might have panicked.

My finger was still pulling back from the bell when the door opened. I expected to see Linda bounce out, carrying her horn, smiling, ready for an evening of football, music, cruising around, and ending up at the local drive-in. The last chime of the bell was just fading away when I realized that it wasn't Linda at the door but a huge, towering, sort of scowling man – *the father*. I must say that I was not a small guy, already six two, but he seemed to loom over me, his eyes narrowing, his mouth already set in what looked like an expression of disapproval. He stood there, just looking silently at me for what seemed like several minutes. Then he looked over my shoulder to inspect my car, the baby blue 1951 convertible, The Humility

Machine, my pride and sometimes joy, which for that brief day or two in time actually seemed to be running fine.

Finally he said, "Linda's not ready yet. You might as well come in and sit down."

By now really nervous, I perched on the edge of the sofa he indicated and tried to relax. He sat opposite me in a large chair and began, skipping any chitchat about the weather or other innocuous topics and cutting straight to the chase. The interrogation that followed was thorough and to the point. Name. Age. Where I lived. How I knew Linda. How long I'd known Linda. How well I knew Linda. What my father did for a living. What my mother did. Whether I had brothers and sisters. Where we went to church. Where my grandparents lived. There wasn't anything alarming about the questions as such, but the deep, resonant voice in which they were uttered seemed to vibrate up and down my spine. Then, there were his eyes, blue with a tendency to narrow at my answers. (I didn't realize blue eyes could be beady until that night.)

Then came the first question I found really problematic, having learned already that a guy's attitude on this topic tended to put him on one side or another of a hard-to-cross divide in maledom.

Him: *You play any sports?*

Me: *No sir, not really.*

Him: *Really?*

Me: *No sir, not since I was a little kid.* (This didn't seem to be going well, it seemed to me.)

Him: *You have any hobbies?*

Me: *Yes, sir.*

Him: *What?*

Me: (with trepidation) *Well mainly model railroading.*

Him: *Model railroading?*

Me: *Yeah...I mean, yes sir.* (I was alarmed that his expression began to change.)

Him: *Do you know anything about real railroads?*

Me: *Yes sir, I know a good bit, I guess.* (His expression changed further – this was getting weird.)

Him: *Do you know that steam engine under cover near the fair-grounds?*

Me: *Yeah, I mean, yes sir. You mean that 2-8-2 that used to run on the Seaboard?*

Him: (after a short silence and further facial adjustment) *You actually know about wheel arrangements on steam locomotives?*

Me: (gaining some nerve) *Sure, I have a 4-4-0, a 2-6-2 and an 0-4-0 in my collection now.*

Him: *How did you get interested in railroads?*

Me: *I guess I always have been – my grandfather worked on a railroad when he was a young man before he went to work for the steel corporation.*

Him: *Your grandfather worked for the steel corporation? Doing what?*

Me: *He was an accountant.*

Him: *Well, if this doesn't beat all. I work in the rail-transportation department at the steel corporation. And my father probably worked for the same railroad as your grandfather.*

Me: *Well, I've always been a train watcher of sorts.*

Him: (smiling, at last) *I guess I had better see what's holding up that girl or you might be late.*

Me: *Yeah, maybe so. Thanks.*

My voice sounded weak, as if all the air had been sucked out of me. As he rose, I became aware that my sphincter muscles had tightened up, and my hands felt sweaty. The guy was frightening. Even so, it occurred to me, I was alive and still here, so I must have said *something* right. I just hoped I could get it right again, assuming there was an "again."

Just then Linda came into the living room, wearing the heavy blue-and-orange band uniform and holding her horn case. She looked very official in a way that I did not associate with first dates, which tended to be frilly and "best-dressy" in nature. Still, she looked good, and after my grilling (even though it did seem to have gone OK in the end) I was more than ready to take off. As we were heading for the door, she glanced at me and then at her father, an odd look on her face. We walked toward the car, me now in charge of the horn, and I glanced over my shoulder. Her father still stood in the door, smiling in the glow of the porch light.

"Has Daddy been asking you questions?" she whispered. Once in the car, she wanted to know what kind of questions, explaining, "He can be tough."

"Is that normal around here? The questions I mean?"

"Well," she said, "I'm afraid it is. Any boy who gets around the house, even if he's just carrying my books home from school or anything, gets the treatment. He usually scares them half to death. I should have warned you." She looked at me. "You don't look scared. Weren't you intimidated by him?"

"Yeah, a little. He's a big guy, not exactly friendly at first."

She thought for a moment and then looked at me more thoughtfully as the car began to move slowly down her street. "I've never seen him smile at anyone I've dated."

"I guess we have some things in common," I ventured.

"Like what?"

"Well, I guess maybe railroad stuff."

"Oh no," she groaned. "Not another one. You don't go looking for places where railroads used to run, do you?"

"Well, I'd rather watch a train actually running, especially steam-powered ones," I said. "I think trains are interesting."

"Oh, now I see why he was acting so differently. You're a railroad nut, just like him." Her tone was resigned, and it seemed to me that she did not sound particularly pleased. Wasn't she relieved that her father hadn't managed to scare me off, or worse?

By this time we were at the stadium, ready to part company for the duration of the game, she off to the band seats and I to settle down a row or two behind. It was a typical late-October evening, very cool and damp with a foggy mist hanging over the stadium, making all the seats clammy. The whole situation was pretty uncomfortable, and our team's performance didn't help anything. From the beginning, as usual, it was clear even to me, not a football follower, that we were to be totally routed, one of those 56-6 scores in which we specialized, the other side usually allowing us one touchdown (field goal not included) for the sake of good sportsmanship. Not that this gesture would gain them any points toward getting the "coveted" Good Sportsmanship Cup – we were developing a perpetual lock on that award, which traditionally went to the team with the worst record that had not actually murdered a member of the opposing team while losing. (Oddly enough, our team had some good players – including a couple who went on to college coaching and even to the pros – but evidently no game plan and absolutely no luck.)

Anyway, there we were, down something like 42-0 when halftime rolled around, poor Linda stuck in the middle of one of the smallest bands ever to take to the field (twenty-four when all of them showed up, which they usually didn't). Except for me and a couple of other embarrassed boosters, most of the people on our side of the stands didn't even seem to notice that our band was trudging around the field toward the end zone, getting in position for the halftime show.

The opposing team that night was a regional powerhouse from a school that required all students not in the ROTC who didn't play football or some other varsity sport to be in the band or cheerleader or majorette squads, which meant that they fielded a band so large that they couldn't all line up in the end zone in preparation for their performance but had to spill out onto the no-man's-land between the field and the bleachers, wrapping around the curved end of the field almost to the fifty-yard line. As they formed sharply defined rows, their cadre of drummers – alone more numerous than our entire band – beating the time, Linda and her fellow sufferers, led by what had to be the most lackadaisical band director in high-school history, walked in a single defeated-looking row into the other end zone to await their turn on the field. The other band's show consisted of an assortment of the latest hits, to which they did a choreographed dance routine even as they played, swinging their instruments high and low, their tall, braided hats bobbing and weaving in perfect precision. Fronting them were about twenty fully plumed majorettes in skin-tight, minimal costumes, led by a drum major, as well as a large flag squad in kilts who twirled their banners continuously. Their program concluded, this monster crowd of players, twirlers and barely clad high-steppers marched smartly off to a loudly executed rat-a-tat-tat and the cheers of the crowd, including more than a few from our side. It had been quite a show.

Then there was a sound of a different sort, not music exactly, but not exactly not music either. Looking toward the end zone where our band had been waiting, we could see that instruments had been raised to lips and the two snare drummers were hitting at their drums with sticks. Something was going on, but it was so faint that those of us in the stands (it was an unfortunately large stadium where even big-time college teams sometimes played) could barely hear it. Still playing, the little group, which on that night numbered about twenty, with a dozen flannel-clad majorettes in front, marched gamely from the end zone toward the fifty-yard line. There they stopped, lowered their instruments and waited for a signal from the band director, who stood before them in an ill-fitting uniform, his shoulders sagging. After the show we'd just seen, maybe he was embarrassed to start the program, I thought. Linda had already told me that he wouldn't let the band practice on the high-school field for more than an hour a week and that they were really bad at marching. As for their playing, in spite of the fact that a couple of the players later went on to professional or semi-professional careers as musicians, what they produced at school assemblies was pretty rotten, barely recognizable in fact. It was unlikely that tonight would be any better.

The silence continued for an uncomfortably long period. Across the way, the other band was almost back to its sitting area. On both sides of the stadium, people trudged up the steps on their way to refreshment stands. I was tempted to go myself. It was cold, the steam rising from the paper cups of watery hot chocolate looked appealing, and I could always do with a Goo Goo Cluster, a peanut, marshmallow and chocolate candy that was a recent addition to the local offerings. Something told me, however, that I'd better tough it out until our band did whatever it was going to do and came off field. Then I'd go get some chocolate and candy for Linda too.

The only problem was that the band wasn't doing anything.

Nothing was happening. Mr. Harris, the band director, simply stood there, his back to us, his arms at his side. People began to notice, including people who previously had paid no attention to what was going on before us. Even from where I sat, I could see the band members beginning to glance sideways at one another, obviously wondering what was going on. Then, at last, Mr. Harris wearily raised his baton, and our part of the show had begun. At least, it appeared that it had. The volume remained so low that all we could hear in the stands were the high points from several John Philip Sousa marches and one apparently heartfelt rendition of *Sonny Boy*, for which the majorettes pulled forth large green handkerchiefs from the pockets of their matronly marching costumes and ostentatiously patted their eyes. Even to a sixteen-year-old, the show was embarrassing, beyond ridicule, but at last it ended and the band began to straggle downfield, back toward the safety of the end zone. They were so bad that the usual catcalls from the opponents were silenced, and the other band applauded and waved their stylish headgear, presumably out of sympathy for fellow musicians in pain.

I was trying to figure out what to say, but Linda saved me the trouble. When I brought her a hot chocolate and a Goo Goo, she didn't even refer to the debacle, but in an ordinary, obviously undisturbed tone thanked me, adding that she was freezing. Evidently, being embarrassed was nothing new to the members of the band, thanks to Mr. Harris. The really stupid thing about the band director was that he wouldn't let any of the band members leave before the game was over (by time, not score, as the latter had happened early on), but he also wouldn't let them play anything. They were allowed only to sit on the cold, unpadded seats, holding their cold, silent instruments as the opposing team put the final nails in our team's coffin, so to speak. Only when the clock ran out and the crowd began to stream out of the stadium were the band members allowed to return their instruments to their cases and leave. Mr. Harris's bad attitude was apparently why there were so few people in the band – the majority had cleared out long before.

Still, all things must end, even lousy football games, and this one did too. I could finally collect Linda, take over the horn case, and hurry her to the car to begin the evening's real entertainment. Once behind the wheel, I headed to the then-favorite hangout in town for high schoolers. It was a drive-in and radio-station combination through whose crowded parking lot it seemed that every teenager in town tried to cruise at least once during the evening, to show off their cars and dates. We were lucky enough to get an actual parking space, in a slot on the edge of the lot, a little out of the main automotive-parade area, but still within a respectably with-it zone. The menus, posted on large billboards on each side of the elevated radio booth, displayed many choices, varying wildly in price. My confidence in the amount of cash I had ebbed steadily throughout the evening – those hot chocolates and Goo Goo Clusters had been more expensive than I'd anticipated, especially when cold and boredom had prompted me to offer a second round. I began to worry about expenses. Since we'd never been out before, I didn't know what Linda might order, so I suggested that the milk shakes (thirty cents) were especially good and the ice cream sundae (twenty-five cents) even better.

Still studying the menu, she began to take off her uniform tie. The tie flung over her shoulder, the wide, stiff leather belt quickly following, she turned her attention to the dozen or so heavily embossed metal buttons of her jacket. "I'm burning up in this uniform," she said apologetically.

"Uh, yeah," I replied, watching as she tossed the jacket into the rear seat, torn between encouraging her to order cheap and continuing to enjoy the sight of her throwing her clothes around.

"You know," she said thoughtfully, her eyes still on the menu, "I'm really hungry. I think I'll start with a BLT and fries and then some ice cream to cool off."

As she spoke, I was madly adding (BLT – thirty five cents, fries – fifteen cents, ice cream – twenty five cents), and then she suggested, as a finishing touch, that we split a king-size chocolate malt (thirty cents). Uh oh, I was already down $1.05 and I hadn't ordered anything for me. Just then I saw the item I both wanted and needed, simultaneously tasty and cheap, a chili dog for twenty cents. That made $1.25, within my budget. I had about four dollars in my pocket, but I needed to get my week's worth of gas on the way home (twenty-six cents a gallon). I issued a mental thanks that she hadn't wanted the fried shrimp ($1 for the small order). If she had, I'd have been sunk, or at least reduced to cadging gas money off my dad, not a pleasant undertaking.

Still flooded with relief, I trudged off to the order window of the self-serve establishment to get our food. All the while I was away, I kept wondering how much more of the band uniform would be in the back seat when I returned. Unfortunately, no further stripping had taken place when I got back and handed her the tray. The interior of the car, however, had taken on the unforgettable aroma of wet wool uniform, to which was now added the overpowering scent of hot grease and chili – quite a heady perfume.

Suddenly I was really hungry too, and it was good to sit in my damp, dark convertible hideaway (the weather had forced me to keep the top up), chewing on what had to be the best chili dog ever, next to the girl I wanted to be with, who seemed equally happy to be with me. She even shared the fries, always a good sign.

It didn't even spoil the mood when she looked at me over the straw in her share of the malt and said, "Another railroad nut, huh? My grandfather, my father, my Uncle Frank and now you – why do I always seem to end up surrounded by railroads?"

I took this to be a good sign, and was sure of it when we parted company at her doorstep.

CHAPTER THIRTY- TWO

TUBBY AND THE FLOORLESS PLYMOUTH

My growing interest in girls, particularly in Linda, the girl from Mr. Bauman's chemistry class, did not end my old friendships (although it did limit the time available for guy things). Given the fact that most of the boys I knew either had, like me, recently gotten their first cars or were about to, a lot of what we did revolved around vehicles. And the kind of car, or even its condition, didn't affect our willingness to be absorbed in one another's wheels.

Take the business of Tubby's floorless Plymouth. I'd known Tubby since third grade, when he moved into the neighborhood and began school with us. The first day of school that September, the teacher asked any new students to stand and introduce themselves. A couple of new kids stood and did as they were told with no particular interest on their part or ours. The third to rise was Tubby. Tubby was big for his age and – though no more than a little overweight – definitely fell into the category of a fat kid in our estimation, and about twenty-five evil little minds were churning out possible nicknames with which to taunt him. As he stood up to his full height with his back to the window, however, the newcomer proclaimed, 'My name is Milton Watson . . . but everybody calls me Tubby." Then he grinned. We sat in shocked silence. He had double-crossed us. He had taken away our fun. From that day onward, he was one of us. Much to everyone's surprise, Tubby grew into a big, tall non-fat teenager, a class leader, in fact. Always friendly, he and I became even better acquainted when we entered Scouting together.

The floorless Plymouth was Tubby's first car. His father owned a repair shop for anything that used a small gasoline engine – lawn mowers, motorbikes, outboard motors, go-carts, and sometimes an automobile. One fateful day in 1956, a man rattled into the gravel lot in front of the shop in a very rough-looking 1949 Plymouth four-door sedan, which he wanted Mr. Watson to listen to in order to render his expert opinion regarding its engine. Mr. Watson listened, poked under the hood, slid underneath, and came out with a look of abject sadness.

The Plymouth owner sucked on his Lucky, blew out a plume of smoke, and said, "Whatcha you think, Cecil?"

Cecil, Mr. Watson, shuffled his steel-toed work boots in the gravel and said, "Butch – she's a goner." Butch said indignantly, "Goner? She's got miles left to go!"

"Yeah, right," Mr. Watson said. "But you ain't got the money needed to get her right."

"That's true," Butch conceded. "I'll leave her here for now and see if I can raise some cash – I'll get back to you." No one – at least no one connected with Mr. Watson's repair shop – ever saw Butch again. After a month or two, Mr. Watson contacted Butch's brother, who hadn't heard from him either, but who did have the title to the Plymouth, which he sold to Mr. Watson for $25.00.

Thus began Tubby's education in auto mechanics, for Mr. Watson informed him that the Plymouth was to be his car if he wanted to put in the work to get it in better running condition (with his father's help, of course).

The car – whose front and back bench seats would between them accommodate six – was by no means a thing of beauty, its original (we think) black finish having weathered into a crusty, soot-like, mottled gray with touches of rust for contrast, but it was wheeled transport, well worth a rescue effort. After two or three months labor and who knows how many parts, Mr. Watson declared it – even with its cracked windshield – roadworthy.

Tubby was on the road! The rest of our group was happy for him, a not-totally-unselfish reaction since the more of us who had cars, the better. You never knew whose car was going to grind to a halt next, so another car in our communal stable was a plus, even one as homely as this.

The first "ride" Tubby gave the guys was to a football game one cold November night. The usual method of gathering a group for an outing was to pick each one up in relation to his nearness to the driver. This meant that I was the first to be collected, so I automatically got the shotgun seat up front, a development that later proved more than lucky. Jeff and Lee were next, collected where they waited at Lee's house – which is where the trouble began. Guys, of course, didn't like to sit three in the front, so Jeff and Lee jumped into the back seat, at which point the dynamic shifted radically. As they stepped in, one on each side, their feet went right through the rusted-out floor boards. (It was fortunate that they

hadn't made one of those running-jumping-into-a-car-in-motion maneuvers or there would have been dire consequences.) As it was, since the car was stopped, they were left standing on the street but yet in the car.

Because all of the work had been concentrated on the engine, transmission and brakes, leaving the aesthetics of the Plymouth's interior and exterior uncared for, no one had been in the back seat, so no one had guessed what would happen when young male feet hit the floor and encountered this trap waiting to be sprung.

Once their initial shock had dissipated somewhat, Jeff and Lee began to argue with each other and curse Tubby. Each one wanted to come up front with us. Three on a seat, maybe, but four? Never! Tubby was owner and driver, but I was first in. No way was I giving up my seat. The two latecomers had to perch up on the back seat with their knees pulled up to their chins in a fetal position for the trip to the stadium. Not only was this position uncomfortable, it was freezing cold. The icy, wet wind whipped up from the road mixed with a whiff of burned oil from the wheezing engine right up through the two gaping holes in the floor.

Everyone in our group begged Tubby to do something about this inadvertent air conditioning, but he said he needed to get the radio and heater working first. After a few breezy outings, Jeff and I (Boy Scouts both and therefore always prepared) measured the holes and cut two plywood panels to cover the abyss. These panels weren't strong enough to stand on, but did finally cut off some of the air flow and that scary view of highway zipping by inches away from our feet.

Tubby actually loved that old rusty wreck, as we all loved our own, but sometimes love is blind, especially if you never have to sit in the back.

CHAPTER THIRTY-THREE

DRIVE-INS, MOVIE & OTHERWISE

Once I got my car, my baby-blue heartbreaker, my roaming area included the usual lineup of drive-in restaurants, burger drive-ins, ice cream drive-ins and even a drive-in doughnut joint. There were also several drive-in movies, but only a quarter of an hour away we had the absolute best and most unique one of all, Auto Movies No. One.

It was the original drive-in movie in the area, hence the No. One name. What made it so unusual was its physical layout, which could best be described as an amphitheater for cars. Imagine a steep semi-circular hillside terraced in a series of sweeping curves, each curve wide enough to accommodate parked cars with enough space behind for the road. The parked cars all pointed toward the screen, which was centered in an opposite curve of the hillside, with the projector building on the same incline as the cars, about halfway up the hill. The concession stand was located off to the right side of the hill.

The last feature was a major reason for this particular outdoor theater's popularity among teenaged food afficionados, for the jolly lady who ran it made the world's best corn dogs. Not made ahead to lie around under hot lights and grow soggy,  but dipped and fried only when ordered. Wow, there was nothing else like those succulent mustard-smeared delights, especially on a cold double-feature night.

Good as the concession stand was, however, it was only the number-two reason to go to Auto Movies No. One. The primary reason for the theater's popularity was the parking arrangement necessitated by the terraced hillside location. To keep cars from rolling forward over the ten-to-twelve-foot drop onto the next row of moviegoers in *their* cars, there was a solid metal-panel fence about four feet high. Of course, this makes sense safety-wise, but the crowning glory had to be the even higher solid fences *between* each parking space. In other words, each car had a three-sided hideaway with almost complete privacy. While not a layout to appeal to the Legion of Decency, much less Planned Parenthood, it struck panting teenagers as the best possible arrangement. Unfortunately, the relative relaxation provided by the privacy of the stalls could have an unsought effect. Couples sometimes fell asleep, to be awakened only by the lights coming on in the wee hours of the morning. More than a few curfews were missed in this way and kids grounded for what seemed like life. (It happened to Linda and me once, but luckily all the parents involved were fast asleep when we returned home.)

There were about six other drive-in movies in the county area, but they were of the standard configuration. Some even had playgrounds located down front for the little moviegoers who became bored with Doris Day or Debbie Reynolds.

The casual nature of drive-ins did have a tendency to turn them into family outings and – being the gentleman I was brought up to be – I sometimes found myself backed into a corner and forced (strongly encouraged?) to take Linda's boisterous younger sisters along on a drive-in movie date. This was not what a sixteen-year-old guy would call the perfect evening. They talked incessantly, teased me nonstop, and forced me to get out every five minutes so they could go to the concession stand or restroom (the convertible was, of course, a two-door). The concession-stand trips provided them with ammunition to harass me further. One time they returned with about fifty packets of sugar, which they proceeded to tear open and dump into the floor of the rear seat. Another time, they ate so much popcorn that one of them threatened to get sick all over everything if I didn't get her some ice cream to "calm" her stomach. More than once, they dumped ice down the neck of my shirt. Worst of all, when we tried to make them behave they were prone to break into endless choruses of *Ninety-nine Bottles of Beer on the Wall* or the dreaded *Frère Jacques*.

The worst of these sister outings involved my engraved, much-in-style gold ID bracelet. I didn't normally like jewelry, but for some reason, this had caught my fancy, and I had worn it for a short-enough period of time that I was still pleasantly conscious of its weight as it slid around my skinny wrist. On this particular night, after about half an hour of being bugged about it, I removed the bracelet so that the girls in the back seat could examine it. Upon being handed the bracelet, one of them promptly dangled it out the window, laughed, lost her grip, and exclaimed with heartfelt horror, "I didn't mean to drop it, honest!"

I got out and looked around. The situation was not promising. For one thing, I didn't have a flashlight or lighter and the drive-in lighting wasn't very good, meaning I couldn't see much of anything in the area around the car, which was undoubtedly where the bracelet now lay. I walked slowly around the vehicle, half bent over, examining the ground as best I could. Nothing. If I wanted the bracelet back (and I did), there was nothing for it but to drop to my hands and knees and begin to inch my way around the gravel pavement, reaching up under the car as far as I could. Somewhat to my surprise, as they worked their way through the sticky, gritty oiliness, my fingers finally found what I was looking for. By that time, of course, my shirt sleeves were pretty much ruined, grime was ground into my pant knees, and my hands were streaked with black grease and God knows what else. I was in no mood to finish the movie. Over the protests of the back-seat girls, Linda and I decided to head home. All the way back, the sisters apologized. They didn't even poke at me as I drove, usually one of their favorite pastimes. It was almost worth it, but just almost.

Drive-in movies were optional, as were most drive-in restaurants. The only drive-in in the city that you *had* to go to was the Sky Tower, which was a combination drive-in and radio station. Everyone between the ages of sixteen and twenty, at least everyone who knew what was what, made it a point to go there with their dates on the weekend to be seen by everyone else who'd come there for the same purpose. The place had its attractions – the food and the radio DJ for starters – but the principal reason to go was to show off your car and the fact that a living, breathing girl was in it with you. The parking lot was literally alive with cars, moving slowly around and through its lanes and parking spaces, some trying to park, others just cruising, all of them tuned to the DJ's frequency.

My best time at the Sky Tower was the Friday night I won ten silver dollars. I'd taken Linda there for a sundae earlier and had filled out a request slip, probably for something like *Party Doll* by Buddy Knox, a favorite of mine at the time. Once the slips were filled out, you sent them to the radio tower booth, and your song was played. Later that night, long after I'd taken Linda home and returned home myself, the DJ reminded everyone of the contest and then drew my slip from all the slips submitted. I heard about my win from a buddy named Tommy, who was listening to the station. He called me about 12:30. My parents were not amused, especially when they learned that I had to be at the Sky Tower within half an hour to collect my win, or forfeit.

Tommy lived on the route to the drive-in, so I picked him up on the fly. Of course, the prize was halfway across town, and to make it I really had to put The Humility Machine into race mode, hoping that it could take the pressure and also that the cops were elsewhere. (They usually hung out near the drive-in just to stop speeders like me.) We made it there with about four minutes to spare, raced up the steps to the booth and rang the entrance bell. I had to identify myself to get the money, but it was worth the race against time. I mean, I could buy a lot of gas with that ten bucks. Even with the lousy mileage I got in The Humility Machine, a world-champion gas guzzler, that was worth at least 300 miles of running around.

The gas, however, would come later. That night was for celebration, and Tommy and I spent some of the ten on a couple of extra-thick chocolate malts. After all, if he hadn't called me, I might not even have known I'd won, and I certainly wouldn't have made it to the Sky Tower in time. What a friend.

CHAPTER THIRTY-FOUR

RIDING THE RAILS – SORT OF

The Keller brothers were good kids to be friends with. Apart from the fact that Joe and Jack were all-around good guys, their father owned a construction company that was headquartered in an area between their house and the main railroad line through the neighborhood. This meant that we teenagers could hang out in and around the storage sheds, garages and shops.

One area we were particularly fond of was the truck shed. We nearly all had cars of our own (including The Humility Machine) by this time, the spring of my junior year, but the idea of fixing up one of Mr. Keller's old trucks for exploring the backwoods began to obsess us. Out there, on the edge of our known urban environment, there were all sorts of decrepit, no-longer-used industrial facilities, many no longer accessible by public road. Their unavailability, plus the vague atmosphere of ghost town that hung over them, was probably why we found the idea of being able to reach them so appealing, especially if it could be done in a vehicle more suited to "over the river and through the woods" driving.

The first hurdle was to get Mr. Keller to agree to give his boys one of the junkers that was past use by his company. After a week or so of wheedling, he gave in and allocated a 1947 Dodge pickup to our project. Our first job was to strip it down to the essentials. With a crew of about six teenaged boys armed with wrenches, crowbars and hammers, the truck was quickly converted into a lean, mean puddle jumper. The first thing to go were the doors – we felt we needed quick access. Next, the fenders – both front and rear – were removed. With this model truck, this meant the headlights went away with the front fenders. Mr. Keller said no to a headlight-less vehicle. He didn't want to get in trouble with the police. So we rigged two lights from an old dump truck onto the front bumper of the Dodge. We now had what we wanted – a doorless, fenderless pickup truck that was what we referred to as a NTL (nothing to lose) vehicle.

When the body work was complete, the mechanical fixup began. The truck would run, but barely. After a few afternoons, some new sparkplugs and a little assistance from the company mechanic, Bud, we were ready to roll. Our initial plan was to hit some back roads in the county that led up into the low ridge of mountains south of town, for it was there that we would find many of the abandoned mines and processing facilities that were our target.

Some of this was just normal kid curiosity about areas that had been off limits throughout our lifetime. Some of it related to the spirit of the times. This was the Cold War era. A lot of people were convinced it was just a matter of time before the Russians either dropped "the bomb" on the U.S. or actually invaded. In school, from about 1950 on, kids went through emergency drills in which we were taught to duck under our desks or behind sofas in the event of an air-raid alarm or huge explosion, as this almost certainly meant the Russians had dropped the atom bomb in the area and we had to take all precautions. There were some pretty specific rules involved. When we came out from our hiding places, we were to eat only food and beverages in secure packaging throughout the bomb attack. If you'd opened that package of crackers before the bomb fell, for example, you'd better not eat them, but a package around which the wrapping was still intact was okay, ditto open vs. unopened bottles of colas. As for the adults, those who took the Russian threat most seriously devised various strategies in anticipation of what they felt was almost certainly coming. Some people built bomb shelters in their back yards; others bought property far away from cities and built survival shacks. These retreats were stocked with cots, canned food and bot-tled beverages, as well as with first-aid supplies, extra clothing, special goggles, and even gas masks. Goofy teenagers like us definitely saw ourselves as the most-reliable line of defense, and we were always on the lookout for natural last stands against the invaders. The grownups might not have a handle on what to do to get rid of those Russians, but leave it to us! We teens would save the day.

So we set out to get a good look at some of these old industrial ghost sites, most still owned by the companies that had once operated them but by this time unused for many years or even decades. We thought we might have to take a couple of detours through the woods to get from the public roads to the old private roads that detailed maps showed. Almost at once, however, we became aware that the roads leading to the old mining and processing sites – including the private company roads that had once criss-crossed the areas – were, for all practical purposes, gone, either washed away or grown up to a degree that even our NTL vehicle would find impossible going. About half an hour after that, further exploration showed us that the railroad right-of-ways always found

in such areas still existed. Some of the site-specific spurs were abandoned and in rough shape, but some of the feeders for main lines were still obviously active. So, the lack of roads would be no obstacle. We could reach almost any of the disused industrial sites, even the mines, by means of the raiload tracks.

This was terrific, we thought, and over several visits, bouncing over the crossties, we reached more than a dozen of these derelict sites. Once there, we mostly just poked around the building ruins, but sometimes we were stupid enough to venture into the mine shafts themselves. We never went too far in because we did have some basic self-preservation instincts. Everywhere we went, we seriously considered the merits of this location or that as the best place to make a stand or even just to wait out whatever was coming.

Using active main-line rails for our outings, even occasionally, was the dumbest thing we were doing. Anything to do with putting yourself in close proximity to a locomotive is dumb, because the train – the heaviest thing around and with momentum on its side – is *always* gonna win that confrontation. It was particularly dumb in this case because we couldn't hear a train coming from any distance because of the noise, the shatteringly loud clattering, clanging, and thudding that the old Dodge truck, its muffler already about shot, caused as it bounded and jounced along, two of its wheels between the rails and the other two bouncing along the edge of the roadbed. Even without that to distract us, our heads reverberated with the sound of our teeth rattling as the truck hurtled over the crossties.

Once we reached our day's destination (it was usually a Sunday afternoon), we always enjoyed ourselves, but this sort of rail riding had its limitations. One was that we couldn't cross most bridges and trestles because they were too narrow for the truck, two of whose wheels were always halfway off the track. Also, foolhardy as we were, we didn't dare venture into a tunnel on an active line. However, we did run through a couple of short ones on an obviously disused line. The fun we were having seemed worth the risk.

If we'd gotten hurt or stranded, we'd have had a long way to go for help. No one's parents knew exactly where we were. Most of us had been sixteen for almost a year or even more, and they were used to our being gone for hours as we aimlessly drove about. Mr. Keller may have guessed that we were up to something a little more adventurous than usual, but, if so, he never asked specifically and none of us volunteered information. Nobody, after all, was interested in being grounded for life, which almost certainly would have been the result of full parental knowledge of our whereabouts. It crossed my mind – and I'm sure the minds of at least a couple of the others – that some of what we were doing had crossed over into a previously unexplored danger zone, but we were teenaged boys and our desire to have fun and equally strong compulsion to impress one another won out.

The incident that brought us to our senses occurred late one fall day while four or five of us were roaring back to town, laughing and with lots of shouting back and forth between the cab and the guys riding on the truck bed. That day we were on a very active section of double-track, main-line railroad. We passed a line of stationary freight cars on the right-hand track and decided that – once past them – we could safely use that track for the first leg of our rail-running. As we bumped along around a curve out of sight of the freight cars, we suddenly realized that the double tracks converged into one, but we sailed on anyway. In a few minutes, the guys in the bed of the truck began beating on the top of the cab and yelling something. Guys were always pounding and yelling on these outings, but this time, almost immediately, the yelling was mixed with a low moaning sound that soon became the wail of a diesel-locomotive horn. About 300 yards behind us was an oncoming train. The yelling then spread to us in the cab. Jack, who was driving, began to look for a way to get quickly off the tracks without flipping us over. He had to slow down to ease the right-hand wheels over the rail, so we could angle down the embankment. We'd gotten off the tracks just in time. As the truck slid to a dusty stop below the right of way, the lead engine roared by, horn blasting, the engineer waving his fist at us and screaming something we couldn't hear but understood perfectly.

We sat there in the ditch while the train passed, scared to death. If we could have gone back to the point in time where we'd gotten onto the main-line track, we'd have done it, but all the wishing in the world wouldn't make that possible. There was no way out of this spot without getting back on the tracks. After considering our options, including hiking back to the public road, hitching a ride to the nearest phone, and allowing somebody's parents to rescue us with the hassle *that* would involve, all of us voted to get back to a real road in any way possible. We piled out of the truck and, slipping and sliding, we pushed it up the embankment and onto the tracks, heading back the way we came. At the first dirt road crossing, we left the railroad to the trains and agreed that there would be no more riding the rails.

The Dodge truck was still fun, and we continued to roar around public roads in it until Mr. Keller pulled the plug on our transportation. He said the insurance premiums on his company vehicles had gotten too high and he was going to drop the coverage on the older trucks, which meant no more street driving. Maybe that was all there was to it. Maybe he got wind of some of our exploits. We never knew. He never said anything else about it, and we didn't have the nerve to ask. Soon after, he sold three of the older vehicles – including our rail-rider – for scrap, but at least it had had a bit of excitement before its day was done.

CHAPTER THIRTY-FIVE

THE COOL GUYS IN THE BASEMENT

"You still play with toy trains?"

Even when I was seventeen, this question had already begun to aggravate me.

Maybe because I knew it didn't really matter what I answered. People who don't understand the difference in toy trains and model railroads will probably never see the difference. Little kids played with toy trains – wooden push jobs and metal or plastic windups. Anyone over five who stayed interested in trains, had to make a serious investment in both time and money that went far beyond simple play. The usual first step was O-gauge stuff, like Lionel and American Flyer, with all of their wonderful specialty cars and accessories. If you stayed hooked, you then typically went into HO gauge. I had followed that route. I was twelve when my interest in O gauge began to wane and I became fascinated with HO's smaller size and enhanced detail. I packed up my O-gauge layout, emptying the sunroom, and sold it to finance my initial forays into HO.

The biggest drawback of the gauge shift was that I lost dibs on the sunroom. Even as I was negotiating the sale of the O-gauge stuff, my parents were picking out paint colors, furniture, and a new television set for what they now intended would become their TV-viewing lounge. Which meant that my first HO layout was tucked into the garage. When that became too inconvenient, I gave up part of my bedroom to it.

Finding HO-gauge gear was something of a challenge. Toy shops didn't always carry it. My local variety store stocked some items but not enough to quench my appetite for more and better equipment. In fact, the hobby shop that I frequented as a teenager was about the only one in the city that had an area dedicated to model railroading exclusively. The shop had come into being a few years earlier. At first we'd all thought it would be competition to Mack's Sports, the shop owned by my parents' friends, but it soon became apparent that Mack's would keep its sports monopoly and the newer hobby shop would leave the sports gear alone and specialize in pure toys or models.

This pleased me because I felt loyalty to Mack's, but I liked the newer shop too. It had a helpful clerk named Marvin who worked part time in the railroad aisle. He and I became friendly on my regular Saturday visits, and after a couple of months, he invited me to visit the railroad layout in his home. This layout, he said, was a club affair. Members gathered in his basement to work on what was turning out to be a rather extensive and complicated railroad with varied scenery, complex track arrangements, and a seriously comprehensive assortment of equipment. Other than at the fair, I'd never seen a really big HO layout, and I was blown away on my first visit to it and the rather loose-knit "club" that had created it.

I suppose I was being vetted. They probably wanted to see if I was a serious modeler. I must have passed inspection because, over coffee and cookies after the evening's session, I was asked if I would like to join. There were dues, but of a small amount that I could easily pay from my part-time grocery-store wages. Besides, the money was for a good cause, going into a fund to purchase supplies.

This was a varied group that, in addition to me, the only student, included a postal worker, an eye surgeon, an architect, an insurance adjuster, and a heating-and-air-conditioning engineer.

The architect, Jim, had designed the amazing multi-level structure and track plan. The eye surgeon, Dr. Grey, specialized in intricate track and switch construction, for which he used his surgical magnifying glasses and a closely guarded little bag of instruments of unknown origin. John, the HVAC engineer, built plaster mountains and timber bridges. Elliott, the insurance adjuster, was our circuit-wiring go-to guy. Marvin, the postal worker and part-time hobby-store clerk, was the woodworking specialist.

My specialty turned out to be was what was called "super detailing." I would add tiny details to the buildings and scenery. For example, I painted "Jesus Saves" on the bench outside one of the small-town stations, put the figure of a bride and groom on the back platform of a passenger car, and applied other little touches of reality. I also did what is known as "weathering," which is the aging and dirtying of buildings, rail cars, and engines for added realism. Having something too new and shiny was my signal to attack with dulling paint, chalk and bottled "grime."

Meeting these HO-gauge experts led me in another direction – working on real railroad equipment, for some of them were also members of the National Railway Historical Society. The local NRHS chapter had been collecting rolling stock, mostly outdated industrial gear from railroads and heavy industry, all of it in various stages of disrepair. The NRHS was relying on its membership to volunteer the grunt work to bring the engines and cars back to some semblance of decent appearance and, if possible, running condition.

These full-size "toys" were stored on a convenient spur track adjacent to the main line running through downtown.

Upon joining the Society, my first work project was the exact opposite of "weathering." It was the painting and lettering of a real railroad caboose. The scheme was shiny and red, with white lettering. Painting the red was relatively easy; hand detailing the white logo and other necessary markings put my art competence to the test. This was very different from detailing I'd done on my own tiny rolling stock. Painting the seven-foot-diameter logo on both sides of a thirty-foot-long caboose took about three weekend sessions. Somewhat to my embarrassment, it went on long enough to attract the attention of a newspaper photographer who surprised me up a ladder painting away. That was one caboose I didn't want to see get "weathered."

Something I really enjoyed about NRHS membership was the chance to go on "fan" trips. These consisted basically of a bunch of crazy guys either riding behind a steam engine in an old passenger car or chasing alongside the tracks on a highway in a car, trying to get that perfect photo. If you were lucky, you had an understanding wife or girl friend to handle the driving so you could focus on the important stuff.

Since Linda didn't have a driver's license, I was out of luck, but at least she rode shotgun and didn't seem to mind anymore that I was, like her father, grandfathers, and uncles, just another railroad nut.

CHAPTER THIRTY-SIX

MY FIRST NEW CAR

I loved my baby-blue '51 convertible. I mean, I literally *loved* it. I liked how everybody would look at it when I stopped for a light or a stop sign. I relished how the guys often seemed to prefer riding in it to any of the other cars to which any of us had access. I would look out the side windows of our house just to catch a glimpse of it sitting in the driveway. The car certainly enabled my dating pattern of going to eat at a suburban drive-in, followed by an hour or so of driving around, after which we'd go back to Linda's house and fend off her kid sisters. Not that the convertible was perfect every minute. That top still caused problems, usually when I least expected them, as in what I came to think of as the soggy-date episode.

Linda and I had by now been dating for several months, long enough that I could go up to her front door and push the bell without getting a sinking feeling in the pit of my stomach at the thought of her father opening the door. We'd been having a good time, but it had all been casual, teenage-type stuff, and it seemed to me that it was time to up the ante by incorporating a fine-dining element. She said that sounded like fun. So when I approached her house this particular night, I felt very sophisticated. I was wearing a sports jacket and dress slacks, with shoes polished so brightly they almost glittered when I walked. I'd also put a special polish on the car and given its interior a good cleaning. I'd checked the weather, and the forecast was for continued clear skies with less than a 20 percent chance of rain, making it possible to have the convertible top down. I'd had a particularly good tip weekend bagging groceries, and had plenty of money in my pocket for the intended entertainment of dinner at the best cafeteria downtown, to be followed by a first-run movie at one of the nearby theaters.

I rang the bell with confidence, greeted Linda's father with what I felt was exactly the right degree of friendliness mixed with respect, and took Linda's elbow to do the gentlemanly assist down the steps of her porch. As her father watched approvingly (I know because I looked back), I kept a light touch on her elbow and opened the door of the '51. It was a beautiful night: warm but not hot, a slight breeze, stars and a big moon overhead, and not a cloud in sight. When I turned the ignition key, Andy Williams was just beginning to sing *Canadian Sunset*. More into Elvis, The Platters, and a new group headed by Buddy Holly called The Crickets, I wasn't exactly an Andy Williams fan, but on that night that music might have been programmed for my mood.

It took about twenty minutes to drive downtown, maybe the most perfect twenty minutes ever in the convertible. It didn't make the funny clicking sound from the front of the vehicle when I braked. It didn't make the usual clunking noise when I shifted from first to second. It didn't even run rough when I was idling at a light or stop sign. It was as if the car knew this was a special evening and was doing its absolute best to cooperate.

Downtown, we parked on the street near the cafeteria. I especially liked this cafeteria because it had historically themed murals on the walls and its steam tables were encased in dark oak paneling. It wasn't as big as some of the others in town, but its food always seemed to be better. The meal was everything I hoped it would be, and we lingered over it and talked in a way that wouldn't have been possible sitting in my car at the drive-in.

"I think we need to come here again," I said in my most adult fashion as we walked out the door into the beautiful night, and was thrilled when Linda immediately agreed.

We'd discovered that both of us were horror fans, and *The Curse of Frankenstein* had opened that week. It was playing at the State, the biggest movie theater in town, only a couple of blocks away, and we decided to walk.

It wasn't quite show time, and there was a line, which wasn't as much of a downer at the State as it would have been anywhere else, for this theater had the ticket booth at the front under the marquee, behind which was a long, covered corridor past glass-encased lobby cards in the walls advertising coming attractions. We inched along, discussing which of those movies would be fun to see and giggling at things we overheard in the line. After about ten minutes, we finally made it inside, into the high, ornate lobby past an enormous and very fancy refreshment stand, which we agreed we didn't need since we'd just had such a good meal and were anticipating going after the movie to our favorite ice-cream parlor. Inside the theater proper, we got exactly the seats I preferred, about twenty rows back from the screen in the center section downstairs.

Man, I enjoyed that movie, especially the heavy handholding that accompanied it. Linda seemed to feel the same way. After it was over and the lights came on, I couldn't have felt much better about anything as we edged along with the crowd into the lengthy corridor and made our way back out to the street. It was then, as we approached the underside of the large marquee, that I realized something was terribly, horribly wrong. It was raining. No, that's inadequate. It was *pouring* and evidently had been for a while, for the streets were running with water to curb height. I was stunned. My car! My sport coat! Her crisp flowered summer dress! What a catastrophe!

I had no umbrella, of course, so I asked Linda to wait under the marquee while I ran for the car. By the time I sloshed the last block to my blue baby, I was soaked. And so was the car. When I opened the door, about two inches of water poured out. I then had to do the manual top-lift-and-latch movements, a process complicated by the fact that I was almost blinded by the continuing rain because my glasses were not only wet, but fogged over. Top finally up, I drove back to the theater, thinking that at least things would be all right now, and then it suddenly hit me – my date would have to sit on the soggy seat with a puddle of dirty water around her feet. Plans for an after-movie banana split had to be abandoned. There was nothing to do but head to her house and call it a night. Obviously, there were no romantic moments in the damp car or at her door, and I wasn't in the mood to come in and drip over her parents' floors. Water sloshed around my shoes all the way home.

I'd had the car for a little over a year at that point. There was nothing I would have liked better than to get the top operative again, but that was so far out of my financial league there was no point even in dreaming about it. I pretty much accepted that the manual top raising and lowering were to be forever. That may have been the first crack in my adoration of my sweet little '51.

The second crack was probably the night after work when, bound for the drive-in to meet some buddies, I ran a yellow light at the same time as a guy coming from my left. We almost missed each other, but not quite. For all its mechanical quirks, the '51 was pretty sturdy, and the damage to my left-front bumper and left headlight seemed relatively minor. I figured that the guys I hung out with could probably help me fix most of it or at least help me find a replacement headlight rim at a junkyard. As for the other car, all it had was a minor dent, so the two of us agreed to call it even and go on our way without doing anything rash like calling the cops.

The other car left, and I resumed my drive-in run. All of a sudden, I realized I couldn't turn left. The accident had damaged the steering mechanism, probably a broken tie rod, I guessed. This part of the city was laid out in a grid pattern with no one-way streets, fortunate since I was going to have to figure out how to get home making only right-hand turns. Home was about three miles west, but with the mathematical puzzle route I had to devise, it was at least twice that.

I did eventually get home, but the damage turned out to be not so minor. In fact, the repairs to the steering, new headlight rim, and touchup paint took all my pay and tips for two weekends. There was nothing unusual in that. The convertible and I seemed to have an implicit understanding. I earned money, and the car required it. That car always knew how much and how often I had funds.

My parents had been making noises for months about how maybe I needed a more-dependable vehicle, but I'd pretended not to hear. I *loved* my little blue beauty. Then, on the night of an especially big date, the '51 died on me again, and I had to borrow my father's Buick Roadmaster, a perfectly respectable car, even a nice car, but built along the lines of a comfortable Sherman tank, definitely not the car a guy wants to collect his girl friend in. I told my parents the next day that maybe they were right, but I didn't see how I could afford a better car. It turned out that they weren't thinking of a better car, but a *new* car, one with no issues whatsoever, and that they were willing to co-sign the note and even help with the payments if need be. (They were evidently getting tired of picking me up and having the car towed from the various places in which it had broken down when I was by myself.)

Once on board, I started to get enthusiastic, and I discovered that nothing in my car experience to that point beat the feeling of walking into a dealership and driving out in a brand-new car of your own. Especially if it's your *first* new car.

I thought my first Ford was cute, but this new one was gorgeous – a 1957, shiny black Ford Fairlane hardtop, well worth the $77 monthly payment that I'd have to clear at my grocery-store job. Best of all, I wouldn't have to spend any money on it for the foreseeable future. And I didn't, at least not for repairs; then, two months in, the first transformation impulse hit me. That car *had* to have a set of 1957 Mercury fender skirts. For some reason, the available Ford fender skirts didn't have the style that this black vision needed. Monetary considerations meant that buying new was out of the question, so this decision led to my spending weeks scouring the city's junk yards and used-parts emporiums before a pair of the Mercury skirts finally turned up. They were, unfortunately, pastel green. This meant that, in addition to the cost of the skirts (and this was a popular item, making it - even used - not cheap), I had to pay to have them painted to match my black car. It was worth every penny. Once installed, the skirts enhanced the Fairlane's long, graceful lines. The quest had been more than worth it.

The second urge toward transformation involved "lowering," which was just what it sounds like. I added lowering blocks between the rear springs and the axel. The combination of lowering and adding the Mercury skirts created a totally hot effect – you couldn't even see the rear wheels at all, making the Fairlane look powerful, like an automotive rocket straining to move forward.

Still, it seemed to me, the look was not quite *right*. It took just minutes to realize that the problem had to do with the wheel covers. The standard Ford wheel covers didn't measure up to the car's new hotness. It was clear that what I needed now were some covers that would complement the evolving image. This was not a decision to be made lightly. After looking around for a few weeks, I settled on 1957 Plymouth wheel covers. Their shape – convex, spun to a point – spoke to my design sensibility. True, their attachments weren't an easy fit for the Ford wheel rims, and I had to jerry-rig them on. Still, they looked *good*. And at least I only needed two since the rear wheels were covered by the Mercury skirts.

Then, one night, coming home from a football game, I learned why you shouldn't mix car parts from different manufacturers. As I was rolling down the right-hand lane of an intown four-lane road, I heard a jarring "clang." The left-front wheel cover had come off. I pulled to the curb so I could jump out and retrieve it; but, just as I opened the door, that damned Plymouth wheel cover came zipping up alongside the car. Far from falling victim to passing traffic, it had caught up with me, where it promptly ricocheted off my newly painted fender skirt, leaving – courtesy of its design-worthy shape – a line of circular scratches along its entire length. The stupid thing then careened across two lanes of traffic, where it was squashed by a bus.

Design sensibility would have to be expressed in some other way, I decided. It was back to the standard Ford wheel covers with the compatible clips. At least, I was able to get a couple of bucks for the single Plymouth cover that remained intact.

It was about that time that it hit me that I was spending almost as much on goodies for the new car as I had keeping the old one running, and for what? The wheel covers hadn't worked out, and the lowered Ford's tendency to scrape when rolling over so much as a piece of wadded paper forced me to remove the lowering blocks. These aborted experiments led me – reluctantly – to a decision that surprised me (not to mention my parents): I would abandon all thought of customization and enjoy the '57's reliability.

The car's size – it felt about twice as big as my baby-blue convertible – provided a bonus in the form of a Mafia-sized trunk. This came in handy when Linda and I – both history buffs – would take off on day trips into the surrounding countryside, looking for interesting old towns, houses, graveyards, and the occasional abandoned railroad station. On many of these trips, we were going into deep country, devoid of restaurants or any other place to eat, so we always carried assorted snacks and an enormous picnic lunch in a big straw hamper. Since we never knew where we'd end up eating – a park with picnic tables (and maybe even a shelter if we were lucky) or a cleared spot on the side of the road – we also carried various necessities: quilt, folding chairs; umbrella, etc. The size of the trunk absorbed it all with enough room left over to haul two or three times as much again.

Having a new car with a pristine interior meant a never-ending fight against muddy feet, food spillage, smoking, and rough-housing. Unlike the upholstery in my baby-blue convertible, the Fairlane's was not vinyl but faintly textured cloth in a sedate dove gray and black. Very susceptible to stains and tears. Unfortunately, to keep my romantic life in balance I sometimes had to take my girlfriend's spoiled dog (a well-marked beagle named Socrates) along on our outings, and Socrates liked to eat. He was especially partial to ice cream, so whenever we went to our favorite ice-cream drive-in, Socrates came along. This establishment was shaped like a giant igloo with a sort of icicle-encrusted portico jutting out front under which sat a life-sized polar bear formed in white concrete. It looked cool even

on the hottest day. Once at the drive-in, the drill was that I ordered giant chocolate malts for us and a small vanilla cone for Sock, as he was known to his intimates. It was challenging to drink my malt while holding Sock's cone over the back seat for him. I tried to keep it over the floor mat because, in his enthusiasm, he usually managed to lick the scoop off and I had already had to clean the seat on several occasions. Fond as I was of Sock, I won't pretend I was comfortable with this routine, but he was a nice dog and, anyway, this earned me major brownie points. Ah, what we do for love.

Another plus for this car over my baby-blue convertible was the large bench seat and column-mounted manual gear shift. I say "plus" on these two features because of the increased room they provided for enhanced enjoyment of those drive-in double features, critical for teenage romance when both the teenagers are movie buffs.

Not that the column-mounted gear shift was an inevitable aid to romance. There was one especially awkward time when, in spite of the brownie points accumulated by my attentions to Sock, it almost cost me my girl. It all began with her father. He thought she should learn to drive a manual-shift car and that I could be trusted to be the one to teach her, in my new car. It didn't occur to me to ask him why he didn't teach her in *his* new car.

The big experiment started out innocently enough. It was a sunny Sunday afternoon, warm but not hot. Flowers were blooming, birds were singing, and Buddy Holly was on the radio. I had put some thought into the proper location for this first lesson, and the winding, traffic-free roads of the biggest local cemetery struck me as a good place to start. I pulled through its heavy gates and turned over the wheel. Things went OK at first. In fact, as long as she was rolling gently along in first, things were fine. Shifting to second was a little rough, but still satisfactory. Road conditions in the cemetery, i.e, curves and the calming effect of all those tombstones, kept our speed down to the point where shifting into third wasn't necessary.

I felt emboldened. This had gone fairly well, so I encouraged her to ease out into the real traffic world, where in this area on a weekend there were few cars and no one in any particular hurry. Everything continued OK until we were caught at a traffic light about three blocks from the cemetery. With some prompting, she managed the clutching and braking with no more than a couple of minor lurches. When the light changed, I told her to hold the clutch in and shift into first gear. It didn't go well. It didn't go well for some time. I can still remember that awful sound – *grind, grind, grind*. Oh no! *She was about to strip the gears in my new car!*

"No, no, no," I yelled. "Clutch, clutch, push in the damned clutch like I told you!"

Big mistake. Given the circumstances, this was not the prudent tone to take. Instead of responding as I'd expected, she put the car in neutral, set the emergency brake just as I'd shown her, and turned to me, her fair skin now a bright pink, her hazel eyes hostile.

"I don't want to do this any more," she snapped.

The image of her father's face rose before me. He'd trusted me to do this important thing, and I was failing.

"Don't give up," I pleaded. "We can go back to the cemetery and drive around some more there."

"No," she snapped. "I don't want to go back to the cemetery. I don't want to go anywhere. I don't care if I ever learn to drive, and certainly not with you. Either you get out and come over here, or I'll get out and come over there."

Without my noticing, while we were having this discussion,

traffic had, of course, picked up, and a line of cars was now behind us. Horns began to sound. The stubborn set of her chin remained firmly in place, and I recognized the inevitable.

"Don't get out," I capitulated. "I'll come over there."

I dreaded having to tell her father how it had gone. Oddly enough, he didn't seem surprised. But it didn't affect my relationship with him. In fact, a few years later, after college and the Army, he and I drove to Colorado together, in a puke-green Volkswagen Karmann Ghia, to ride the Denver & Rio Grande Railroad, but that's another story.

CHAPTER THIRTY-SEVEN

TIME TRIPPING

I grew up, with the usual sequence of events that this process involved at the time: College, Army, Career, Marriage, Moving Away. As I changed and matured, so did the crowd that had been around for all of my life.

The drifting apart had begun long before, of course; I just hadn't noticed. Even after Linda and I moved away, I didn't realize how distant the past was from what the present was becoming because my parents stayed in the neighborhood, close to the hospital where my mother now managed the gift shop, and she kept me up to date on what was happening back home. I knew when Vernon went to work for NASA as an engineer with a specialty so classified he couldn't even tell his mother what it was. When Freddie graduated from law school and passed the bar. When Annie – after two kids and some bad experiences – divorced her creep of a husband because he turned out to be a wife abuser. When a kid up the street went to Viet-

nam and didn't come back. When one old buddy had twins, and another lost his wife to acute appendicitis. When the wild boy across the street, who'd grown up to be a social worker helping troubled teens, disappeared while driving back from his job in California to visit his mother. When Roy committed suicide.

Roy? Roy, who had guts enough to face down the biggest, meanest bullies in school? Roy, who'd outwitted every teacher we ever had? Roy, the ultimate kid entrepreneur? Roy, who'd turned into a handsome man about to become a stockbroker the last time we'd seen him? Suicide? No way. But it was true. He'd hung himself. Just twenty-five years old. A sad and – it turned out later – badly abused boy who'd become a sad and vulnerable man unable to find enough bearable in life to justify its continuing.

As for me, life did go on. I made a career out of art. I stopped being quite so skinny. The Army helped with that, I was 6'2" and 135 pounds when I went in and fifty pounds heavier when I came out, a gain that has been all too easy to maintain (and even exceed). Linda and I discovered the "joys" of restoring old houses. We established a very different pattern of life in a very different place. For years, we went back home at least once a month for a long weekend and, at first, spent a week there at Christmas and usually another in the summer. Even so, with two sets of parents to visit, as well as grandparents and assorted other relatives, all of whom lived as far apart as possible it seemed to us, there was rarely time to seek out old routines, and bit by bit it all fell away. Partly because everybody started moving away. Linda's parents were among the earliest, even before we married. They'd long felt cramped in the small post-World War II house they'd bought in 1947 and then enlarged a couple of times. They built a larger house in a nice new subdivision further away from the industrial sites that were the source of the area's wealth. They were soon followed by others who were lured by the same things that had lured them – bigger houses, bigger yards, winding roads, the illusion of country with the convenience of new systems and ready access to major highways.

By the time my father died, twenty-four years after I graduated from high school, almost none of the neighbors I'd known while growing up were still around. More than the identity of the neighbors had changed; so had the demographics, a direct result of changing economic realities. The industrial base that had provided the best-paid employment had diminished steadily. This affected not only those employees (and the people of the next generation who would have become employees) but also the businesses they would have patronized and *their* employees. What this meant for the old neighborhood, at least for my street, was that almost everyone who bought from those bound for the deeper suburbs was retired. These retirees were there not to be within easy driving distance of the big industrial employers and their vendors but because they wanted a nice area in which to live but either couldn't afford or didn't want to spend the money on one of the feature-loaded houses in the newer developments. They were there also because they didn't have to care about the quality of the local schools, which, sadly, had tanked, in part because a deteriorating tax base had made it hard for the city to spend enough money to keep them up to standard, but in part also due to the fact that all those often-exceptional women who'd taught us belonged to the last generation of females with few other career choices. The newcomers were as house proud as the old. The houses remained well-maintained, the yards just as neat as those I knew, but no kids played movie games across the back yards and none roamed the alleys, looking for useful junk.

My mother continued to live for several years in the house where she'd spent all her married life, going to the same church and shopping in the same stores even as she watched the last of the old neighbors leave and welcomed the new. She was, however, a practical woman, and when her health changed, she knew the time had come to relinquish the responsibilities of house upkeep. She chose a condominium building with a doorman and concierge, called the moving company, and put her home of fifty-three years on the market. When she re-located, I lost my last tie to the old neighborhood, but I recall it – and the experiences that I had while growing up there – with fondness of startling intensity.

When I look back on my boyhood in that time and that place, what I think of most is how free and safe it seemed, which was, of course, what provided the sense of security within which we all had so much fun. No matter how screwy the situation, you always knew there was – probably closer than you thought – an adult around to provide aid if needed. It was a rich and full growing up, with few regrets – well except for crashing into the curb on the Donald Duck bicycle (the bone fragments in my left elbow still twinge) and releasing that poor goldfish Vernon won at the fair into the even-then polluted waters of the creek on the way home.

I guess there is one other thing I regret, at least sort of. I continued to enjoy Scouting, and rose through the ranks until 1954 when I moved into the Explorer Scout Division. There I got as far as Star Scout ranking, two below the exalted Eagle status. In all, I won eighteen merit badges and remained active in scouting until I turned sixteen. I probably would have stayed in longer for more good times with the guys, but I was weak. Cars – and then girls – beckoned, and that was that. But maybe I was too easily distracted, because the experience obviously mattered a lot to me. I've still got souvenirs from Scouting days, saved by my mother: my sash with the merit badges; the bird I carved on a campout; and the woodburning project with the troop name.

I've got other souvenirs of boyhood that have less-pleasant connotations. The doctors say, barring some pretty serious cosmetic surgery, I'll always have the scar on my nose from the Nazi-Dagger episode – thanks for nothing, Patrick. I'm pretty sure the aversion to the smell of Pinesol will be lifelong as well.

I hung onto a couple of other childhood souvenirs that I would just as soon have lost. I remain permanently weak in math and totally unable to identify the parts of a sentence. Fortunately, the diagramming of sentences hasn't been required as a life skill. Math, however, is a very different issue, and I've struggled many times with simple equations. Thank goodness for calculators.

As for a souvenir I wish I still had? How about my baby-blue beauty, the '51 Ford convertible? I'd like to have it around, if only just to look at, as I doubt I could afford its inevitable ability to require more money than I have in order to keep it running. And it'd be fun to have the newspaper clipping of the photograph showing me at work on that seven-foot-high logo on the shiny red caboose.

I still like a lot of the same things. Cherry Cokes. Multi-layered cakes with lots of frosting. Chocolate-and-nut candy bars. Fireworks. The smell of wet wool (capable even now of providing an instant semi-sexual thrill). Donald Duck comics. Working on projects (even without the benefit of a NASA-bound science nut to help). Old books. And, of course, the "naked ladies," in and out of showers. Thank you, Roy – wherever you are – and I'm sorry none of us realized how bad you had it.

One thing I have never done, thanks to childhood experience, is to order *anything* from any TV ad. (I kept, and still keep, half of a blue Borax wagon in my model-building scrap box to remind me why.)

I do, however, continue to "play with trains," and I remain mostly faithful to HO gauge (although N and G have their charms and I've even backslid into O territory a couple of times). I still have fun on Halloween. A few years ago, at an auction of redundant props held by the local community theater, I acquired the Tiny Tim tombstone from *A Christmas Carol*, which has proven to be a highly useful part of the seasonal setting, per-

fect when combined with a dirt mound and candles for simulating the proper front-yard atmosphere for neighborhood trick-or-treaters.

I continue to draw on everything. Something else I can still do that surprises me is approximate the classic writing style that Miss Poore tried so hard to teach us. I have to be careful – and it helps to have ruled lines – but it's amazing how trippingly those neat ascenders and descenders continue to flow from my pen. One thing has changed. Now when I travel, I know what I'm seeing and I remember it, unlike that long-ago trip out west for which my mother held such high hopes. Which is not to say that kids shouldn't be taken on trips. I can see how the right trip at the right time could give a kid the memory of a lifetime. Unfortunately we probably only know what that would have been when we're well past the age of having it done for us. (For me, I think it would have been Goodrich Castle in Wales when I was about ten and capable of spending days clambering over its crumbling ramparts with an imaginary sword and shield.)

There are things about boyhood that make me wonder. What was the green fluid in the wax cola bottles sold by Shepard's

Shoe Shop? Did Vernon ever go onto another boat after Old Leaky? What was in all those Chocolate Soldiers I swilled in such quantities over the years? How did the '51 Ford convertible, my baby-blue beauty, know when I had two cents in my pocket? And did my father subsidize the repairs – in retrospect they seem improbably cheap, even for the time – that his mechanic made? What would my old Lionel layout be worth today? How did I escape serious injury, given all the things Vernon and I used to get into? Remembering some of the stuff that happened, I can't believe I got through my childhood and teen years without losing my life, or at least a finger or two. I really don't count my broken elbow – that was an innocent bike accident not in the category of fooling around with real trains and fireworks. I wonder, most of all, what happened to "Donald" after the crash?

I'd especially like to know how I got through that first interview with "the father." Even in retrospect, it still seems more alarming than any subsequent grilling I had from potential employers, IRS auditors, bankers controlling my business's line of credit, or even gimlet-eyed security men in foreign airports where they take such things seriously.

One of the best things about revisiting boyhood has been the combination of sights and sounds and smells that I had no idea I retained. The delectable, forever-unidentified perfume worn by Miss Manfred, my first art teacher. The wonderful mixture of aromas of shoe polish, leather, candy, pipe-tobacco smoke, and Juicy Fruit gum in Shepard's Shoe Shop. The sound of corn dogs cooking at Auto Movies No. One. The somewhat wheezy honking of my blue beauty's horn. The feel of the wind across my crewcut as Chuck Berry chastised Maybellene and my grandfather's new Mercury cruised sweetly down that distant highway. And, best of all, lying on my back in a grassy clearing beside a lake, staring upward, while a Scout leader used his flashlight to guide us across the nighttime sky. I don't think I could imagine any better introduction to astronomy. I can still see those dippers, archers, bulls, twins, and all their kin. It took my breath away then, and still does.

A lot of what we did back then was free, a product of imagination and effort, but a lot of it cost money, albeit surprisingly small amounts. (It's hard not to be surprised today at what a kid could do with ten dollars then.) Of course, there are things that would have shocked me as a kid if I could have looked into the future. Take the merging of many of the candy-bar companies, which has led to the crosshatching of candy types. The Avalanche, for instance, is essentially a Hershey's-covered Payday. Is that heresy or brilliant improvisation? Today, I'd opt for the latter. I suspect that the kid that I was – something of a purist when it came to candy – would have been outraged. Another thing that would have shocked me is the increase in the use of white chocolate – I always thought that Zero bars were a perversion.

I'd have been even more shocked if I could have looked ahead and seen that the strip shopping malls even then popping up around the fringes of town were the beginning of the end for downtown as a shopping Mecca, an end to be accelerated by shopping centers, big-box stores, mail order, and online retailing. We'd have been especially horrified if anyone had told us, as we sat eating our lunches with Bobby's mother, that not only would the lunch counter go away but so would the big Sears store in which it was located. It wasn't so much that any of us were huge fans, just that Sears had always been a part of our landscape. Most unexpected of all would have been the fact that there are no longer cabooses on trains. Of course, some shocks would have struck me as totally positive – such as the fact that, in 2009, I could access the roster for my 1952 Boy Scout troop online. And how about the fact that I have, thanks to iTunes, a section on my iPod full of all my favorite highway music?

The world has become much more expansive in some ways for kids, but some of the improvements seem to have come at the expense of the kind of homegrown fun we had then. There are, of course, exceptions. One fine afternoon, in the stolid intown neighborhood where I lived for many years, I heard the familiar yet unexpected sound of kids playing war: guttural machine gun noises, juicy explosions of imagined hand grenades, and the rat-a-tat-tat of tinny ricocheting bullets. Across the street I caught a glimpse of two boys zigzagging through the shrubbery in full battle gear. Armed with plastic M-16s, helmets and side arms, they were attacking full tilt at some unseen (by me) enemy. I really wanted to cross over and ask them who they were fighting, but I knew my interruption would not be appreciated and would ruin their fun. I know if some adult had approached Vernon and me in one of our make-believe modes, we would have been either embarrassed or royally pissed off. Still, I'd like to have known what their inspiration was. Ours would have been the movies. Theirs could be any number of things – movies, television, video games, or even books. Still, the inspiration didn't matter, but the fact that the kids were using their imaginations with a riotous display of excess energy.

And some kids still take trick-or-treating as seriously as Vernon and I did. It was Halloween a few years ago, not totally dark but almost past twilight, and kid traffic had already been brisk in my city neighborhood. Ghosts, superheroes, vampires, clowns and assorted well-costumed monsters roamed the streets, and many had already made their way to the porch where I waited in my just-returned-from-the-grave costume, acquired from a really cool shop in Doylestown, Pennsylvania, an area where they know how to do Halloween right. Suddenly, there was a whoop, and a huge horde of elaborately costumed kids ran up the walkway toward me. Behind them trudged a tiny girl, barely big enough to walk. Her fellow trick-or-treaters had already scooped candy from the bucket and were turning to race back to the adult who waited for the group by the sidewalk when the little girl began to toil up the twelve steps to our door. She was wearing a frilly pink tutu, along with a glittery, somewhat askew set of wings and carried, almost dragged, a small treat bag. As I was dropping Hershey Kisses into it, the adult – probably her mother, since she was the smallest of this particular group – called out, "Clarice, hurry up. We need to move on." Clarice turned toward the direction of the sidewalk, stamped her tiny ballet shoe on the step, and shouted, "I not Clarice. I Tinker Bell!" I made encouraging grunting noises and put extra mini candy bars into her bag out of admiration for her determination to stay in character, but she was obviously embarrassed by having her identity blown.

I couldn't help envying Clarice and all the Halloweens she'll have to get her persona just the way she wants it. I also can't help envying, just a little bit, the boy that I was. It was a super boyhood, enabled by a lot of adult generosity and guidance. In retrospect, there were people I wish I'd thanked more. So here goes. Thanks to the guys who introduced me to model railroading as a serious, all-encompassing hobby and, in the process, taught me a lot about professionalism and teamwork. Thanks to our Scout leaders, who gave up so much time and went to so much trouble to indoctrinate a bunch of green boys with the wonders of the wider world. Thanks to Gloria, my young aunt, for making possible that life-defining moment driving my grandfather's new Mercury, the windows down, *Maybellene* blaring on the radio. Thanks to the father of "the girl" for recognizing a kindred spirit. Most of all, thanks to my parents for making that wonderful growing up possible and for balancing freedom, security and opportunity with such grace that I never suspected what had to have been involved. It was the best childhood ever.

The End

About the Book

The Cover

The cover was designed by author Robert G. Hewitt, an award-winning graphic designer and illustrator. **Typography**: main-title – Haettenschweiler 68 pt; subtitle – Gapstown AH 50 pt; author name – Hoefler Txt 30 pt; spine copy – Haettenschweiler 24 pt; and rear-body copy – BodiniEF 14 pt. Photograph, of Robert Hewitt at age 12, is from the author's personal collection.

The Interior

The interior was designed and illustrated by author Robert G. Hewitt, an award-winning graphic designer and illustrator. **Typography**: chapter numbers – Franklin Gothic Heavy 14 pt; chapter names – Haettenschweiler 30 pt; and body copy – Hoefler Txt 12 pt. Photograph of the author's parents June and Buster Hewitt, circa 1938 –two years before his birth, is from the author's personal collection.

Made in the USA
Middletown, DE
11 July 2024